GOD'S EVERLASTING SIGN

GOD'S EVERLASTING SIGN

BY J. L. SHULER

Southern Publishing Association,
Nashville, Tennessee

This book was

Edited by Richard Coffen

Designed by Dean Tucker

Cover photo by Ray Pike

Text set 11/13 Times Roman

Printed on Trade Litho Hibulk

Cover stock: Husky C1S

Acknowledgments

In addition to the King James Version of the Bible, quotations are made from the following translations:

The Emphasised Bible: Rotherham's Translation.

The New English Bible. Copyright, The Delegates of the Oxford University Press and The Syndics of the Cambridge University Press, 1961, 1970. Reprinted by permission.

Printed in U.S.A.

CONTENTS

1

REDISCOVERING A CONNECTING LINK

Sweeping the world, materialism, secularism, and humanism have blotted out the consciousness of God among countless millions. One of the fastest-growing segments of world population has no religion at all.

Thus, A. C. McGiffert says:

"As ever new forces were discovered in nature, and phenomenon after phenomenon formerly traced to divine activity was given a natural explanation, there seemed less and less place left for God and less and less reason to believe in him. *Unless a revolution occurred in the prevalent idea of God and new ways of looking at him were found, the growing skepticism of the age must in course of time become universal.*"—*The Rise of Modern Religious Ideas,* p. 188. Quoted in *Current Christian Thinking,* p. 128. (Italics supplied.)

Most men simply ignore God as irrelevant and meaning-less and go on their way quite unconcerned as to whether God is or is not. And with what result? Man's disrespect for God and His law has mushroomed while morality and spirituality have declined. More than ever before people need a connecting link with God for right guidance.

God has ever sent messages of truth specifically designed to meet man's needs, and in Revelation 14:6-12 He sets forth in capsule form His special instructions for our day. It presents fresh ways of looking at God, ways which answer the errors and growing skepticism of this age. It restores an original connecting link between the true God and man, which nearly all who desire to follow Him have lost sight of.

Strange as it may seem, this forgotten connecting link deals with the two most significant facts for every soul on earth—creation and redemption.

Without creation we would not exist. Without redemp-tion our existence would be useless. Creation and redemp-tion, the two greatest facts in the history of man, tower above all others like the two highest peaks in a mountain range.

Every Christian knows that redemption is vested in the Lord Jesus Christ, but millions of these same Christians do not realize that creation is also vested in Him. They do not understand that Jesus, the Saviour, is also the Creator.

Why this lack of knowledge? Because they remain un-aware of seven New Testament passages which declare Jesus of Bethlehem and Nazareth as the Creator of all. We list the references here and will discuss some of them later. (John 1:10; 1:1-3, 14; Ephesians 3:9; Colossians 1:14-16; 1 Co-rinthians 8:6; Hebrews 1:1-3; 1:8-12.)

Many Christians assume that the Lord Jesus Christ be-gan His existence at His birth in Bethlehem. The truth is, as Christ states in John 17:5, that He existed with the Father before the world was created. In addition to being truly man, He is also truly God, coexistent with God the Father from eternity. (John 1:1-3, 14.) The person who limits Christ's existence from Bethlehem holds a faulty concept similar to that of the man who reckons the size of an iceberg by what is visible only above the surface of the water.

Many think that when they read a "Thus saith the Lord" in the Old Testament, it refers exclusively to something spoken by God the Father, and that they do not read what Christ says until the first book in the New Testament. Such is not the case, however, because all of the Father's dealings with this world have been mediated through His eternal Son —the Lord Jesus Christ. (John 1:18.)

Christ is the Lord who spoke through the Old Testament prophets (1 Peter 1:8-10), and the New Testament identifies Him as the Creator-God of Genesis. Both Christ, the eternal Son, and God, the eternal Father, are the Jehovah of the Old Testament. In John 8:58 Christ calls Himself the I AM—the Lord God of Abraham, Isaac, and Jacob, who spoke to Moses at the burning bush.

Christ the Lord spoke the Ten Commandments at Sinai and wrote them on two tables of stone. Jesus Christ, as God the Son, the Second Person of the Godhead, led the Israelites through the wilderness into Canaan. How tragic that when He united His divinity with humanity and lived among them, the vast majority rejected the very One who had been their God from the time of Abraham.

In creation it is a case of the Father, "*of* whom are all things," and the Lord Jesus Christ, "*by* whom are all things." (See 1 Corinthians 8:6.) The Father allotted to His Son the active role in creation. Thus Christ is the Co-creator of all along with God the Father and God the Holy Spirit. Both creation and redemption are the overall work of the Trinity:

John 1:10, in speaking of Christ as He lived on earth following His first advent, positively asserts that He is the Creator of this world: "He was in the world, and the world was made by him."

The first chapter of Hebrews draws aside the curtain to give us the privilege of listening in on a divine conversation between the Father and the Son. In this conversation the Father refers to His Son as the Lord who made the heavens and the earth. He also ascribes eternal self-existence to Christ. (Hebrews 1:8-12.)

In Ephesians 3:9 we read, "And to make all men see what is the fellowship of the mystery, which from the beginning of the world hath been hid in God, who created all things by Jesus Christ." You can see that this plainly states that the Father created all things by Christ. The context in verses 3 to 11 presents one of the most sublime and assuring truths in the entire Bible. It shows that the creation of all things by Christ constituted part of God's eternal purpose to assure salvation to those who love His Son. Creation and redemption in and through the Son of God are the unfolding of the Godhead's precreation plan concerning humanity. Christ the Son is the Father's delegated Co-worker in the creation of all things and in the redemption and restoration from sin.

The Scriptures reveal that God provided salvation through His Son before the world began. (2 Timothy 1:9; Titus 1:2; Ephesians 1:4, 5; 1 Peter 1:18-20.) Yet only a few know this thrilling truth. When Adam sinned, the Son of God as his Creator became his Redeemer. Thus Revelation 13:8 declares Christ to be "the Lamb slain from the foundation of the world."

When man sinned, no created being could satisfy the claim of God's broken law. Only one equal with God could atone for transgression. Hence, no one but the Creator—

the Son of God—could offer Himself as the sufficient ransom for sinful man. Christ had to be the Creator so that He could become the Saviour when the emergency arose, for the Creator alone can give the sinner a new heart and make him into a new man. Christ is the only Saviour for every soul, because as the Creator He has the creative power needed to regenerate the believer.

Both the Old and New Testaments show that creation and redemption are united in the same Lord (see Isaiah 43:1; 44:24)—our Lord Jesus Christ. The New Testament in three places introduces Christ as both Saviour and Creator of all. (See John 1; Hebrews 1 and 2; Colossians 1:14-16.)

Colossians 1 presents this truth in a striking manner. Verse 14 declares that in Christ we have redemption through His blood. Verse 15 adds that Christ is the image of the invisible God. Then verse 16 presents the basic reason for redemption through Christ. How does it begin? The first word is *for,* which, in this instance, means "because." Redemption comes through Christ, *because* "by him were all things created."

The unity of truth in Christ the Truth (see John 14:6) requires that we truly accept Him as the Creator-Redeemer. Christ cannot be divided. Christ as the Redeemer cannot be separated from Christ the Creator, or vice versa. God has inseparably united creation and redemption in His Son. One demands the other, for God's ultimate purpose in creation is finally realized in redemption.

This means that Jesus, the Son of God, sustains a basic twofold relationship to us. And the supreme, decisive issue facing every person is how he honors his twofold relationship to Christ his Creator and Saviour. Many do not realize that Christ has appointed the keeping of the seventh-day (or Saturday) Sabbath as a distinctive sign whereby we acknowledge that He is our Creator-Redeemer. It forms that needful connecting link between the wondrous Creator-Redeemer and His creatures on earth.

Where do we find this in the Bible? The revelation unfolds with Christ's words in Exodus 20:8-11; Exodus 31: 16, 17; and Ezekiel 20:12, 20.

Exodus 20:1-17 records the Ten Commandments. The divine Lawgiver identifies Himself in verse 2: "I am the Lord," meaning the "I AM"—the self-existing One, the eternal One. (Compare Exodus 3:13, 14.) Christ declared Himself to be the "I AM" when He said, "Before Abraham was, I am." John 8:58. Hence, this phrase in Exodus 20:2 —"I am the Lord"—reveals that Christ gave the Decalogue.

Exodus 20:11 further confirms this by identifying the "Lord thy God" with the Creator of this world: "For in six days the Lord made heaven and earth." The "Lord thy God" of the Decalogue is the Creator. Now, John 1:10 and Ephesians 3:9 clearly establish that the Creator-Lord is the Lord Jesus Christ. These are the commandments of both the Father and the Son.

Now notice what Christ said regarding the day we should keep holy: "Remember the sabbath day, to keep it holy. Six days shalt thou labour, and do all thy work: but the seventh day is the sabbath of the Lord thy God: in it thou shalt not do any work, thou, nor thy son, nor thy daughter, thy manservant, nor thy maidservant, nor thy cattle, nor thy stranger that is within thy gates." Exodus 20:8-10.

Since Christ is "the Lord thy God," who gave this commandment, then, according to Christ's declaration in Exodus 20:10, the seventh day is the Sabbath of the Lord Jesus Christ. It is not the Jewish Sabbath, nor the Adventist Sabbath, but Christ's Sabbath.

Sunday is the first day of the week. Thus, when Christ declares that "the seventh day is the sabbath of the Lord," He settles it that Sunday, the first day, cannot be His Sabbath for Christians. Since the seventh day is Saturday, then according to Christ's command in Exodus 20:8-11, Saturday is the Lord Jesus Christ's Sabbath for Christians. Christ, the Creator, commands the observance of the seventh day in the Ten Commandments. Those who assert that Christ never commanded the keeping of the seventh day are wrong, for they contradict what Christ said when He spoke the Decalogue.

Obviously there is a discrepancy between the keeping of the first day of the week (Sunday) and Christ's command to keep the seventh day; and the only way to correct this discrepancy is to do what Jesus says, to keep the seventh day as His Sabbath for man.

Further, every Christian should heed Christ's threefold reason why the seventh day is His Sabbath for man and should be so observed in preference to any other day. He says, "For [because] in six days the Lord made heaven and earth, the sea, and all that in them is, and rested the seventh day: wherefore the Lord blessed the sabbath day, and hallowed it." Exodus 20:11.

Christ commands us to keep the seventh day in preference to any other day, because *first,* He, as the Creator-God, made the world in the first six days of the first week of time; *second,* He then rested upon the seventh day; and *third,* He hallowed or set apart the seventh day as His holy day for mankind after He had rested upon it way back *in the beginning.*

Most assuredly, some who keep Sunday will argue that Christians need not keep the seventh-day Sabbath. They attempt to show by the Bible that the observance of the seventh day was a Jewish ordinance instituted when the Israelites came out of Egypt and that it ended with the Jewish age at the cross.

This theory does not harmonize with the Scriptures. The

words of the Son of God, the Creator, as recorded in Exodus 20:11; 31:16, 17 show that the seventh day is to be kept holy because of what Christ did at creation some 2,500 years before the Jews came out of Egypt. Genesis 2:3 explains that the Creator blessed and sanctified the seventh day at the close of creation week. In Exodus 20:11 Christ refers to the seventh day as the Sabbath when He thus blessed and hallowed it. He made the Sabbath for man when He made man.

The Scriptures reveal decisive information as to which day we should observe. If a person inserts into the Ten Commandments any of the other six days as constituting the Sabbath of Christ, then the commandment contradicts itself, for it would assert that the Lord rested from creation and worked at creation on the same day. Christ's threefold reason why we should keep the seventh day cannot hold true of any other day except the seventh, the last day of the week. Christ Himself has settled it forever that the seventh day of the week is the only right day to keep.

Also it seems self-evident that this threefold reason for observing the seventh day applies not merely to those Israelites to whom the Lord spoke His law but to every soul on earth today.

Next, let us consider our Lord's words in Exodus 31:16, 17. In verse 16 the Lord mentions His seventh-day Sabbath, and in verse 17 He says, "It is a sign between me and the children of Israel for ever." Then the next word is "for." The Lord again states the reason why the Sabbath is a sign. "For [because] in six days the Lord made heaven and earth, and on the seventh day he rested."

We have seen that in seven places the New Testament identifies this Lord who made the world in six days as the Lord Jesus Christ. Therefore, Exodus 31:16, 17 stands as evidence that the Sabbath is a sign, because the preincarnate

Christ made the earth in six days and rested on the seventh day. *The Sabbath is a sign that Christ is the Creator.*

The Bible further teaches that not only is the Sabbath a sign of Christ the Creator, but it is also a sign of Christ as the Re-creator, or Redeemer. "Moreover also I gave them my sabbaths, to be a sign between me and them, that they might know that I am the Lord that sanctify them." Ezekiel 20:12.

The Lord declares that He gave His Sabbath as a sign so that His people who keep it may remember that He sanctifies them. Thus, *the seventh-day Sabbath is also a sign that Christ is the Sanctifier, or Saviour.*

Such is a natural and necessary arrangement, because God the Father, according to His eternal purpose, allocated creation and redemption to His eternal Son. Since redemption involves re-creation, Christ can be the Saviour only because He is also the Creator.

Hence, the Word of God presents the seventh-day Sabbath as a sign, or token, memorializing both the Creator and Saviour. *Christ the Creator-Redeemer is the heart of the Sabbath.* Keeping the seventh day as Christ has directed signifies that we acknowledge Him as our Creator and our Re-creator. What a high value this places on true Sabbathkeeping! What a holy incentive to keep the Sabbath according to Christ's instructions in His Word!

Understanding the relation between Christ and the Sabbath reveals the divine beauty, the need, and the appropriateness of the seventh-day Sabbath in the Christian life. Just as a beautiful rose is the natural outgrowth of the rosebud, so the observance of the seventh day as the sign that Christ is the Creator-Saviour is the natural outgrowth of accepting Him as our Lord and Redeemer. Surely every Christian will want to accept this sign of Christ, for everyone needs to understand and experience above all else this

Scriptural revelation of the Sabbath as the sign of the Lord
Jesus Christ, the Creator-Redeemer. Why? Because it points
up the *true meaning of the Sabbath as an everlasting sign of
Christ's twofold relationship to humanity.*

Many regard a presentation of the Sabbath as a trouble-
some and unnecessary emphasis upon what they consider of
little or no consequence, and therefore they dismiss Sabbathkeeping as misguided legalism and an outmoded practice. Such reasoning results from their lack of knowledge
regarding the true meaning of the Sabbath as set forth in
the Bible.

Many people think this Sabbath-versus-Sunday issue is
merely a matter of whether one shall rest on Saturday or
Sunday. Hence the prevalent yet erroneous concept that it
makes no difference what day one observes, if any. Reduc-
ing the Sabbath merely to a day of physical rest misses the
real truth in Christ, for it is contrary to how the Sabbath
originated. The everlasting God and Creator never gets
tired or weary. Christ the Creator did not rest on the first
seventh day for physical rest. Rather, He rested spiritually to
make every succeeding seventh day a spiritual rest for man
in joyful contemplation and commemoration of the Lord as
the Creator.

Adam kept his first Sabbath on the first whole day after
God had created him. He knew no physical weariness until
after he sinned. God gave him the Sabbath first of all as a
spiritual rest and as a sign whereby he recognized the Son of
God as his Creator. It was a special way whereby he honored, adored, and worshiped his Maker. It indicated his
allegiance and obedience to the only true God and Supreme
Authority.

After Adam sinned, the Creator became his Redeemer.
Then the Sabbath became a sign of his recognition not only
of Christ as his Creator but also of Christ as his Re-creator,

and it did afford needed physical rest.

The Sabbath, given first to signify his creation in God's image, became a pledge and token of his restoration to that divine image by Christ. Thus, *keeping Christ's Sabbath is inseparably connected with the acceptance of Him as Lord and Saviour*—contrary to the assertion of some Christians that if a person accepts Christ, it makes no difference whether he keeps the true Sabbath or not.

It is supremely essential that every soul rightly honor Christ as Lord and Redeemer. Since true Sabbathkeeping signifies our acceptance of Christ as Creator and Saviour, then it is of basic importance in living for Him. "And hallow my sabbaths; and they shall be a sign between me and you, that ye may know that I am the Lord your God." Ezekiel 20:20.

The appointment for keeping the seventh day stems out of Christ's imcomparable relationship to every person as the Creator and Redeemer. It serves as a necessary connecting link between Christ and His human creatures. Setting aside Christ's Sabbath in favor of another day is tantamount, therefore, to setting aside Christ as Creator and Saviour. In supreme love to Him, we should gladly honor and worship Him as directed by His Sabbath sign.

2

REMEMBER THY CREATOR-REDEEMER

Three words—Remember thy Creator-Redeemer—embrace the real meaning of life, expressing the supreme issue facing every soul. They set forth the destiny-deciding question for every person. They apply even for eternity to all who enter heaven. These three words constitute the background of the Lord's appeal to all. Thus we read in Isaiah 43:1, "But now thus saith the Lord that created thee, O Jacob, and he that formed thee, O Israel, Fear not: for I have redeemed thee, I have called thee by thy name; thou art mine."

Many think that God the Father created man and that His Son redeemed him, but this verse indicates that the same Lord who says, "I have redeemed thee," declares that He had also created. Here is a wonderful Old Testament revelation of Christ the Lord as Creator-Redeemer. (See also Isaiah 44:23, 24.)

We have seen in the previous chapter that the New Testament even more clearly reveals Jesus Christ as the Creator-Redeemer. (See Colossians 1:14-16; Ephesians 3: 6-14; John 1:3, 12-14; Hebrews 1:1-3.) Christ our Creator-Saviour is the very heart of salvation.

The gospel revealed God's precreation plan which determined that His Son should both create and redeem humanity. Hence, Christ sustains this all-important twofold relationship of Creator and Saviour to all people, and every soul settles his own eternal destiny by how he remembers and honors his Creator-Redeemer.

In view of all this, it is altogether logical and necessary that as soon as the Son of God made man, He should provide an effective means whereby, if followed, man would remember his Creator. Genesis 2:3 shows that Christ did provide for this. After He made the world and man in six days, He rested on the seventh day and blessed and sanctified it, or set it apart, to be a continuing memorial of Himself as the Creator.

We need not be uncertain about the Sabbath memorializing the Creator and His creation. In the Ten Commandments Christ commands us to observe the seventh day as His Sabbath because He made the world in six days, then rested on the seventh day and sanctified it for man. (Exodus 20: 8-11.)

The idea that the Sabbath was only for the Jews contradicts Christ, who said, "The sabbath was made for man." Mark 2:27. Man, used here in the generic sense, means all mankind. Hence, no one need fall into the error that the Sabbath is only a Jewish ordinance and that it was not instituted until Moses led the Israelites out of Egypt. It dates back to creation week.

What a day of holy joy the first full day of Adam's existence must have been! In perfect union with his Creator in a spiritual rest, he delightfully contemplated a perfect work in all the world. The Sabbath as a link of love would hold him from week to week in a living contact with the Lord of all life.

Each sanctified seventh day of the week bears the inscription "Remember thy Creator-Redeemer." He who rightly remembers his Creator-Redeemer in genuine Sabbath observance will have no other gods before the Lord. He will obey the other commandments, because he loves God with all his heart, soul, mind, and strength. And when he does this, he will also love his neighbor as himself, thus fulfilling all the law.

It is as important and necessary to keep the Sabbath as it is to remember Christ as the Creator-Redeemer, because it is His everlasting sign, or memorial. Does this mean that the Sabbath will continue for eternity? The Word of God confirms it in prophecy: "For as the new heavens and the new earth, which I will make, shall remain before me, saith the Lord, so shall your seed and your name remain. And it shall come to pass, that from one new moon to another, and from one sabbath to another, shall all flesh come to worship before me, saith the Lord." Isaiah 66:22, 23.

This prophecy concerning the coming new earth, the eternal home of all the redeemed, reveals that the saved will honor the Sabbath through all eternity. Therefore, man's plan of substituting Sunday-keeping for Christ's Sabbath runs contrary to God's plan for Sabbath observance from Paradise lost to Paradise restored.

"This prophecy also speaks of observing new moons in the new earth," some may say, "but Colossians 2:16 states that these ceased at the cross when the Jewish age ended."

Just as the Israelites devoted the new moon or the first day of the month to special religious services, so "from one new moon to another" in the new earth refers to certain special religious services to be held on the first of each month, lacking, of course, any of the abolished features in the ceremonial law. Perhaps there is a connection between Isaiah 66:22, 23 and Revelation 22:1, 2, for the tree of life may present one of its twelve kinds of fruit on the first of each month.

Christ's Sabbath is, therefore, an eternal institution. What a high value this places on observing the seventh day! In the new earth all will be one as are the Father and the Son. All with one heart will observe the Sabbath in eternal recognition of Christ, the Creator of the perfect world in the beginning and the Re-creator of the earth and its people to original perfection. We should gladly keep the Sabbath as part of the operation of divine grace in our lives so that it may do its part to prepare us for entrance into the heavenly land where all will honor it world without end.

In direct opposition to Sabbath observance, the vast majority of Christians keep Sunday in commemoration of Christ's resurrection on that day. They claim that if Christ had not risen from the dead, there would be no salvation for any soul. A dead Saviour could save no one. They argue that it is necessary to keep Sunday to commemorate the Lord's resurrection, thus rendering it the proper honor it deserves.

However, keeping the seventh day as Christ has directed does not detract one iota from the honor due His resurrection. But why single out His resurrection above other equally vital links in the golden chain of salvation? Not a soul could have been saved if He had not left heaven to be born in human flesh. None could have been saved were it not for His sinless life, His vicarious death, and His priestly intercession. Further, without the creation by Christ there would have been no one to save. Keeping Christ's Sabbath as His appointed sign that He is the Creator-Redeemer embraces all these necessary events, for it commemorates the whole of Christ's work.

Does the Bible indicate that Christ the Creator has taken His blessing and sanctification from the seventh day and placed it on any other day in the week? The answer is, No. Therefore we conclude that *the seventh day is still Christ's blessed, sanctified day for man to observe.*

In fact, this blessing and sanctification are nontransferable from the seventh day. Why? Because God conferred these upon the seventh day when He rested on it. His rest can hardly be moved from the seventh day to any of the other six days on which He did not rest. The seventh day must continue forever as Christ's blessed, sanctified day.

Has anyone ever found a text in the Bible which says that we should keep the first day of the week to honor Christ? The Lord gave the Scriptures for our guidance. Wouldn't He, then, have told us in the New Testament to keep the first day in honor of Christ if this were part of His will for us?

The silence of the New Testament regarding the keeping of the first day (or Sunday) implies that uninspired men introduced Sunday worship after the New Testament was written, or after A.D. 100.

Have you noticed that the Book of Acts shows that the same seventh day which was Christ's Sabbath before His death on the cross continued to be His holy day for His people in the decades following His death and resurrection? Acts 13 records a sermon Paul preached to the Jews in their synagogue at Antioch on the Sabbath day around A.D. 45, or some fourteen years after our Lord's resurrection. Notice, too, that the Word of God refers to this meeting-day as *the* Sabbath day. "But when they departed from Perga, they came to Antioch in Pisidia, and went into the synagogue on *the sabbath* day." Acts 13:14.

Surely God's Word would not and *could not* refer to the seventh day (or Saturday) as *the* Sabbath day years after Christ's death and resurrection if the first day (or Sunday) had taken its place.

The Book of Acts furnishes abundant evidence for keeping the Sabbath and in eight different places calls the day of worship the *Sabbath*. (Acts 13:14, 27, 42, 44; 15:21; 16:13; 17:1-3; 18:4.) These texts stand as eightfold evidence that keeping the first day in honor of Christ's resurrection was not part of Christ's plan for His followers.

Christ's death for our sins is central and indispensable in all Christianity. Why, then, should we not keep Friday to properly honor the cross? Every informed Christian will answer, "The Bible does not direct us to do this. We honor His death by receiving Him as our personal Saviour, by being crucified with Him every day so that He can live in us, and by partaking of the bread and wine at the Lord's Supper."

Such an answer harmonizes with the Scriptures. There is no valid reason to keep Friday in honor of His death, because Christ appointed the Lord's Supper to commemorate His crucifixion. Similarly there is no valid reason to keep Sunday in honor of His resurrection. The New Testament says nothing concerning the observance of the first day of the week as a memorial of the resurrection, but there is plain, direct testimony showing that the Lord ordained baptism to memorialize His death, burial, and resurrection. We read in Colossians 2:12, "Buried with him in baptism, wherein also ye are risen with him through the faith of the operation of God, who hath raised him from the dead."

Baptism by immersion declares our faith in Christ's death for our sins and in His burial and resurrection. Baptism serves as a continuing memorial to the resurrection of Christ. We properly honor His resurrection by dying with Christ to sin, by partaking of the power of His resurrection for right living, and by participating in the Biblical mode of baptism by immersion.

Since redemption is re-creation, the same original Sabbath He instituted to commemorate creation also commemorates salvation.

This reveals the falsity of the claim that with the new Christian dispensation it was necessary to turn from the old Sabbath of creation and to keep the first day as an alleged Lord's day in commemoration of redemption. The candid person will recognize that these Scriptural considerations dislodge the very foundation on which so many have built Sunday-keeping.

Here's another consideration. Doesn't a person's birthday or wedding anniversary come on a different day of the week through the cycle of seven years? The answer is, Yes. Also Independence Day, July 4, likewise falls on a different day of the week each year. Christ's resurrection took place on the first day of the week in the year He was crucified, but didn't the recurring anniversary of His resurrection come on a different day of the week each year thereafter like one's birthday or wedding anniversary? It certainly did.

Thus it was not only contrary to the truth in Christ but also futile for men in post-apostolic times to make a weekly memorial of Christ's resurrection on every Sunday when the real anniversary of His resurrection comes only once a year and on a different day of the week each year.

In direct contrast to this, notice the logical and appropriate plan of the Creator and Lawgiver. In the fourth precept of the Ten Commandments, He directs man to use the first six days of each week for work and then to rest on the last day of each week as a commemoration of Christ's work in making the world in the first six days of the first week of time and of His resting on the last day of this same week.

Please mark this well. The Sabbath is the only element

of the calendar enshrined in the Decalogue, because it has moral and spiritual implications not associated with mere dates or historical happenings.

Christ cannot be divided. We must hold to the whole Christ, who is the Creator-Redeemer. The Sabbath, as a sign of creation and redemption, fits into this concept of the whole Christ. But note that when a person omits keeping the seventh day in favor of observing Sunday, *he is attempting to separate Christ the Creator from Christ the Redeemer.* Isn't this a wrong course for a Christian to follow?

Full commitment to Christ includes more than honoring Him as the Lord of redemption. We must also honor Him as the Lord of creation, and we reveal our faith in both His ministries by keeping His Sabbath.

Christ the Truth embodies all saving truths. When a person has the real truth, all his beliefs harmonize in Christ; and if one of his ideas does contradict another, it calls for further investigation and adjustment until the sum total of his beliefs constitutes a harmonious unit.

If a person believes the New Testament teaching that Christ is the Creator and omits keeping the seventh day in favor of keeping Sunday to memorialize redemption, then his own practice contradicts his belief in Christ as the Creator. He is attempting to separate Christ the Creator from Christ the Redeemer.

On the other hand, Christ's seventh-day Sabbath stands for His inseparable role as Creator and Redeemer. You know there is only one true Christ—the Creator-Saviour. So the seventh day, as a sign of the Creator-Redeemer, is the only true Sabbath from the beginning through all the ages and into eternity. It is an everlasting sign of the Creator-Saviour.

3

IN TUNE
WITH
THE HEAD

The Head of all humanity expressed the secret of right living and of a meaningful life in seven words: "Abide in me, and I in you." John 15:4. Our greatest need is to be linked with the Lord Jesus Christ. He said, "He that abideth in me, and I in him, the same bringeth forth much fruit: for without me ye can do nothing." John 15:5.

Your body with the proper action of its different members strikingly illustrates the need of being in tune with the Head. You know also that to enjoy a television or radio, you must tune it with the respective stations. Similarly, Christ the Creator provided an effective means for man to keep in tune with Him. The first Friday sunset Adam saw began the Sabbath. On this first seventh day the Creator rested, and Adam, in union with his Creator, kept this first Sabbath.

Then the Son of God planned for the seventh day to be a holy meeting time between Himself and man. The Sabbath is a cord of love that binds created man to his Creator by affording a closer fellowship with the Lord than on the working days. The original plan of the Sabbath envisioned its perpetual observance as long as the Creator and the created should exist. In keeping with this, the Lord set forth the Sabbath as "a perpetual covenant." (Exodus 31:16, 17.) His purpose can never fail, and thus God's faithful will honor the Sabbath for eternity in the new earth. (Isaiah 66:22, 23.)

When one understands that the Sabbath is a token of God's love as exemplified in creation and redemption, it becomes very precious. Then he happily and gratefully honors and worships the Son of God as the Creator-Redeemer by hallowing the Sabbath. Every soul who accepts the Sabbath as a twofold sign of Jesus fastens himself to the golden chain of obedience that leads to heaven. The effectiveness of true Sabbathkeeping as a link to hold men true to God is manifested in that if everyone since Adam had rightly observed the Sabbath, there wouldn't be an infidel, atheist, idolater, or criminal in the world today.

Adam and Eve lived in perfect harmony with their Creator until they sinned. The secret, then, of keeping in tune with the Head is continual obedience to His commandments. Notice how Jesus emphasized this: "If ye keep my commandments, ye shall abide in my love; even as I have kept my Father's commandments, and abide in his love." John 15:10.

He who knowingly and persistently disobeys any of Christ's commands cannot remain in tune with the Head. Thus He asked, "Why call ye me, Lord, Lord, and do not the things which I say?" Luke 6:46.

The validity of the seventh-day Sabbath for our day ties

into the present-day status of the Ten Commandments. It is evident that if the Decalogue is still binding upon all, then the keeping of the seventh day is also binding upon all. In this case everyone who does not hallow the seventh day transgresses the fourth precept of the Decalogue.

On the other hand, what if the Ten Commandments as given to the Jews expired when the Jewish age ended at the cross? What if a new and different law which omitted the Sabbath commandment superseded them? If this were true, then the keeping of the seventh day is not necessary. Everyone must know the truth from the Bible concerning the law.

Many believe that under the new covenant, after Christ's crucifixion, He ordained a new law to replace the Ten Commandments and that the keeping of a new day—the first day of the week in honor of the resurrection of our Lord—replaced the seventh-day Sabbath of the old covenant. The preceding chapter presented abundant Scriptural evidence to the contrary. However, some may ask, Does the New Testament show that the same Ten Commandments given at Sinai are binding on Christians under the new covenant?

Hebrews 8:8-10 gives us the answer by directly quoting from Jeremiah 31:31-33 in the Old Testament: "For finding fault with them, he saith, Behold, the days come, saith the Lord, when I will make a new covenant with the house of Israel and with the house of Judah."

Notice in verses 10 and 12 what the Lord does with His law of Ten Commandments under the new covenant on behalf of those who accept Christ: "For this is the covenant that I will make with the house of Israel after those days, saith the Lord; I will put my laws into their mind, and write them in their hearts: . . . and their iniquities will I remember no more."

The original verse in Jeremiah 31 which this statement quotes reads, "I will put *my law* in their inward parts, and write it in their hearts." Verse 33.

When God spoke of His law of moral conduct in the days of Jeremiah, He clearly referred to the Decalogue, which He had written on two tables of stone. What did the Lord declare concerning His law of the Ten Commandments under the new covenant? Did He say, "I will give you a new and different law?" No. Did He say, "I will revise My law and give you a new weekly holy day to keep"? No. He said He would write His law upon the hearts of those who enter this new covenant relationship with Christ.

Under the new covenant, the Lord by the Holy Spirit writes upon the renewed hearts of converted persons the same Ten Commandment law that He had formerly written upon the two tables of stone, thus establishing that the seventh-day Sabbath of this Decalogue continues as His holy day for Christians under the new covenant.

Make no mistake about it. *Paul sets forth as the heart of the Christian faith* that which God revealed to Jeremiah as the heart of the new covenant—forgiveness of sin and the Ten Commandments written upon the renewed heart.

All will agree that Christ's twofold role as Creator and Saviour is just as basic under the new covenant as it was under the old covenant. Therefore, the Sabbath, the sign of the Creator-Redeemer, is just as applicable under the new covenant as it was under the old covenant.

The Ten Commandments, as spoken from heaven by the Lord and written by Him on two tables of stone, differed from the ceremonial law of typical ordinances. Hence these Ten Commandments, as God's eternal rule of right, continued after the cross. Paul, James, and John in their epistles refer to the Ten Commandments as a binding rule of conduct upon Christians. (See Ephesians 6:2; Romans 13:8-10; 7:7; 3:31; James 2:10, 11; 1 John 3:4; 2:3, 4.) And, of course, it follows that as surely as this Decalogue is binding, so the keeping of the seventh day continues.

The underlying principles of the Ten Commandments, such as love, honesty, truthfulness, purity, etc., express God's character. They cannot be abolished nor outmoded nor superseded, but they remain as unchanging as is God.

Some may ask, How can you harmonize this with Paul's statement that Christians are not under the law, but under grace? We must settle it once and for all. God's Word, when rightly interpreted, never contradicts itself. When Paul declared that born-again believers "are not under the law, but under grace," he did not contradict what he wrote when he urged Christians to live according to the Ten Commandments.

Paul uses "not under the law, but under grace" in the sense that a Christian does not stand under the condemnation of law, because in Christ he has received full pardon for his transgressions of that law. Along with this, by the grace of God, he receives a new heart, or mind, so that he can and will obey God's commandments.

Thus the Lord said through Ezekiel, "I will take the stony heart out of their flesh, and will give them an heart of flesh: that they may walk in my statutes." Ezekiel 11:19, 20.

Those "not under the law, but under grace" are those who, by the inworking of grace in their lives, are free from the dominion of sin—free from transgressing the law. Thus we read, "For sin shall not have dominion over you: for ye are not under the law, but under grace." Romans 6:14.

It is plain that when a Christian is "not under the law, but under grace," sin has no dominion over him. And what is sin? 1 John 3:4 says, "Sin is the transgression of the law." So, when sin does not have dominion over him, he stands delivered from transgressing the law—in Christ he obeys the law.

All will agree that being under grace does not give any

person the right to steal, lie, swear, or to violate any of the Ten Commandments. Paul discusses this in Romans 6:15: "What then? shall we sin [or transgress the law], because we are not under the law, but under grace?" What is Paul's strong negative answer? "God forbid."

Paul referred to the Gentiles as "them that are without law," because they did not have the written law as did Israel. In this same connection he stated specifically that as a Christian, he was "not without law to God, but under the law to Christ." (1 Corinthians 9:21.) The Greek here literally reads "in law to Christ."

"Under the law to Christ" takes into account that Christ has freed Christians from the ceremonial laws of the Jewish regime. It includes obedience to all the moral and spiritual precepts God gave Moses and all the Ten Commandments as kept by Christ in His earthly life and as proclaimed by His teachings.

"Salvation is only by grace," some retort, "and not by the works of the law. Hence the keeping of the seventh day according to the law is contrary to salvation by grace alone." Such an attitude exemplifies how a half-truth may be more dangerous than completely erroneous teachings. The first part of the statement is true, but the second part is unscriptural.

Sabbath observance by a born-again person is no more contrary to salvation by grace than are kindness, purity, honesty, and truthfulness in obedience to the sixth, seventh, eighth, and ninth commandments. Ezekiel 20:12 sets forth the Sabbath as a sign of sanctification by grace. So, instead of Sabbath observance contradicting free grace, it actually signifies that grace in the Christian's life.

Some conclude from Matthew 22:34-40 that Christ set the Ten Commandments aside in favor of the two commandments of love—love to God with all one's heart and love to one's neighbor as himself. They fail to understand that these two precepts include all the ten in their widest spiritual scope. If a person loves God with all his heart, he will obey the first four. Without this kind of love, he cannot obey them. If he loves his neighbor as himself, he will obey the last six of the commandments. Without such love, he cannot do this. "Therefore love is the fulfilling of the law." Romans 13:10.

The Ten Commandments are a law of love, and whatever service we render to God or man, if it be without love, we have not fulfilled the law. Love should compellingly motivate obedience. True love constrains us from violating any of the ten. Thus, obedience is a link of love that binds us to the Father and the Son. "If you love me, you will keep my commandments." John 14:15, R.S.V. As surely as we love Jesus, we will obey Him. His commandments include all of the ten He spoke from heaven at Sinai and all He set forth in His teachings during His sojourn on earth.

If a person holds back from keeping Christ's commanded seventh day, he needs to pray for more love for his Saviour, for full love makes it easy and delightful. Lack of the requisite love does make Sabbathkeeping hard and burdensome.

Creation and redemption express God's love for man beyond anything else. The Sabbath is Christ's appointed sign that He is the Creator-Redeemer, it stands as a token of God's love, and as we understand its true significance, our observance of it will reveal our love for Him.

Everyone who owns a Bible has Christ's commandments before him, but how few obey them, expecially His command to keep the seventh day! Yet obedience spells out our love for Him. Jesus said, "He that hath my commandments, and keepeth them, he it is that loveth me." John 14:21. In 1 John 5:3 we read, "For this is the love of God, that we keep his commandments: and his commandments are not grievous."

How tragic that many Christians willingly live according to all the Ten Commandments except the one which says, "The seventh day is the sabbath of the Lord." Christ has made His Sabbath the test of obedience to all His commandments. Hence, true Sabbathkeeping distinguishes the obedient from the disobedient. With masterly power Satan has worked to nullify the Sabbath commandment. How vital, therefore, that we, by God's grace, stand on the side of obedience to God's commandments.

The person in tune with Christ will follow His commandments. "Hereby we do know that we know him, if we keep his commandments." 1 John 2:3. But what about the man who professes to follow Christ yet refuses to obey God? "He that saith, I know him, and keepeth not his commandments, is a liar, and the truth is not in him." Verse 4.

Sunday-keeping has no Scriptural connection with creation or redemption through Christ. However, keeping the seventh day harmonizes with the Biblical injunction to honor and worship Christ in His dual and incomparable standing as Lord of creation and redemption. Surely this should suffice to lead every Christian to follow through on his faith and to decide in favor of God's everlasting seventh-day memorial! Indeed, if those good Christians who keep Sunday understood these truths from the Word, they would, in their love for Christ, gladly turn from Sunday-keeping to obey Christ by honoring the seventh day.

How important is it for every soul to obey Christ? We turn to Hebrews 5:9 for the answer: "Being made perfect, he became the author of eternal salvation unto all them that obey him."

Nothing is more important than obeying the Lord Jesus Christ. He declared that the man who hears His teachings and neglects or refuses to obey them is like a foolish man who built his house on the sand. When the storm struck, it collapsed. But the man who hears His words and obeys them is like the wise man who built his house on the rock. It withstood the blast of the storm. (Matthew 7:24-27.)

Every person confronted with God's message of observing the seventh-day Sabbath is like one or the other of these two men. He either obeys or continues to disobey. Either he learns and does, or else he learns and does not act on Christ's command. Surely you want to build on the Rock.

4

IS
YOUR GOD
BIG ENOUGH?

The creation of heaven and earth clearly reveals the omnipotence of Christ our Creator. "Ah Lord God! behold, thou hast made the heaven and the earth by thy great power and stretched out arm, and there is nothing too hard for thee." Jeremiah 32:17.

Jeremiah saw creation as evidence of God's unlimited power. Since the Sabbath is a sign of Christ as the Creator, it also signifies His omnipotence. What a high value this places on observing the seventh day!

It is to the discredit of many Christians that they seem to think their God not big enough to make this world in six ordinary days as mentioned in the Sabbath commandment of Exodus 20:8-11. Keeping the seventh day according to this commandment bears a continuing witness in one's life that the Lord made the earth in six of the same kind of days

He has allotted us for our affairs each week. The Sabbath constitutes a divine answer to the theory of evolution with its millions of years.

The Sabbath, then, is a definite part of—the finishing touch to—God's creation, because He made the Sabbath on the last day of creation week, each day of which consisted of twenty-four hours, even as today.

The evolutionary theory, however, contradicts this. It claims that this world and man evolved through millions of years. Many Christians who attempt to blend creation with evolution claim that these six days of creation week were long periods of time.

If this were the case, then the seventh day on which the Lord rested was also a long period of time which has not yet ended. Thus, there would seem to be no possible ground for keeping the seventh day as a weekly memorial of God's creation and rest, and the devil has endeavored to accomplish this with millions who believe in God.

The Bible says that each of these six days consisted of an evening (a dark part) and a morning (a light part). (See Genesis 1:5, 8, 13, 19, 23, 31.) Whoever heard of an evening and a morning continuing for a thousand or more years? Such talk is Biblically and logically unsound. Creation week consisted of ordinary twenty-four-hour days, as determined by the revolution of the world upon its axis, even as we measure every day now.

If we misconstrue these six days of creation into long periods of time, then we invalidate the Sabbath as a weekly sign of Christ the Creator. Christ's Sabbath perpetually witnesses to the direct creation of man in the image of God and of the making of the world in 144 hours. Thus, the God of truth designed true Sabbathkeeping to serve as an effective bulwark against the errors that have arisen concerning the origin of man and the world.

Can anyone truly keep the seventh day for the reason Christ sets forth in Exodus 20:11 and 31:16, 17 and at the same time subscribe to evolution? When a person keeps the Sabbath as the Lord directs in these texts, he thereby commits himself to the doctrine of the creation of this world in six twenty-four-hour days. A person cannot truly observe the seventh day for the reason Christ specifies in Exodus 20:11 and at the same time deny the direct creation of the world and man in six days as described by Genesis 1.

God's appointed message for this closing age, as set forth in Revelation 14:6-12, calls for all to worship Christ as the Creator. (Verse 7.) Surely, this involves observing His seventh-day Sabbath, because it is Christ's sign of creation —an antidote for Darwinism.

By accepting the evolutionary theory, multitudes of Christians have set aside the first three chapters of Genesis. Yet, as go these first three chapters, so goes the remainder of the Bible, because all that follows these three is an amplification. As a result many no longer regard the Bible as the ultimate standard for determining truth or as a relevant and authentic guide for one's life.

If Darwinism is true, then there was no fall, as described in Genesis 3. If no fall, then the Saviour is meaningless and unnecessary. Any evolutionary theory which denies the fall of man into sin repudiates Christ as the Creator and Saviour. Evolution not only strikes at the Sabbath as a sign of creation, but it also undermines the Sabbath as a sign of redemption.

The wide acceptance of Darwin's theory has produced a baleful harvest of materialism, atheism, humanism, and skepticism. It has led men to think God is unnecessary and useless, but the Sabbath, with its vivid presentation of Christ as our Creator-Saviour, remedies this situation.

The seventh-day Sabbath, as the sign of Christ the

Creator, stands or falls with the six literal days of creation. If we vitiate the sign of Christ as Creator, then we also invalidate the sign of Christ as Redeemer. If the Sabbath command is made void, the Decalogue is also, because the Sabbath precept imparts the authority of the Creator and only true God to the entire law.

The adversary of the truth is aware of this. Hence, from the beginning he has studied to pervert, distort, set aside, conceal, and repudiate the Sabbath. His success is revealed in the fact that the Sabbath is the most misunderstood, opposed, and disregarded of Christ's doctrines.

The theory of evolution represents Satan's scheme to relegate Christ's Sabbath to the scrap pile, to offset God's message for the restoration of the true Sabbath, and to warp the minds of millions so that they cannot accept the Bible Sabbath on the basis of the Lord's command in Exodus 20:8-11.

At the mention of keeping the seventh day according to God's commandments, some object, You don't take into account that we live in an entirely different age from when God proclaimed the Sabbath to the Jews. But Christ has not changed, nor have His Ten Commandments. Christ is still the Creator-Redeemer for every soul, and keeping His Sabbath forms a necessary part of our recognition and worship of Him as such.

Since faith without works is dead (James 2:17), God has provided appropriate ways whereby we may manifest our faith by doing that which He has appointed. Christ's Sabbath commandment certifies that keeping the seventh day is a divinely appointed way whereby we show our faith in the creation of this world in six literal twenty-four-hour days. Therefore, all who believe that Christ created the world in six literal days should reveal their faith by keeping His Sabbath. A Christian vainly believes in creation as recorded in Genesis 1 and 2 if he does not keep the Sabbath.

The Word of God challenges us to stand firm for the six-day creation of Genesis 1 and to show our faith by observing the seventh day or else to believe in the evolutionary theory and thereby repudiate the divinely appointed basis for the Sabbath. Logically, there can be no middle ground.

Not only do some Christians seem to think that their God is not big enough to create this world in six days as described in Scripture, but they fail to understand that their God is also big enough to effect the Incarnation of Jesus Christ so that our Saviour was both divine and human. Thus many Christians deny the deity of Jesus of Nazareth. They laud Him as a good man—perhaps the best man that ever lived—and as a great moral teacher, but they refuse to acknowledge that He was truly God as well as truly man.

Some may ask, What difference does it make whether or not I accept Jesus as the Lord and God-man so long as I follow Him as the best man? Salvation is at stake here. A merely human Christ cannot save anyone. Apart from the Lord there is no Saviour. (Isaiah 43:11.) Jesus told the Jews that if they refused to believe that He was God, they would die in their sins and perish. (John 8:24.)

Only God could create our world. Therefore, the fact that Jesus Christ made the world furnishes sure evidence of His deity. The Bible sets forth the only true God as the Creator of all, in contradistinction to the vast array of false gods, none of which have made the heaven and earth. (Jeremiah 10:10-12; Acts 17:23, 24.)

Exodus 20:8-11; 31:16, 17 and Ezekiel 20:12 point out that Christ has tied the Sabbath to His incomparable standing as the Creator-Sanctifier. Hence, by keeping the seventh day, we continuously acknowledge that Christ is the divine Creator and Redeemer. Indeed, He declares that Sabbath observance is a sign that He is God. "And hallow my sabbaths; and they shall be a sign between me and you, that ye may know that I am the Lord." Ezekiel 20:20. Everyone, therefore, who believes that Christ is Lord should reveal his faith by keeping His Sabbath.

Thousands of ministers and laymen in the various evangelical churches stand steadfastly for the six-day creation week of Genesis 1 and the deity of Jesus. However, as commendable as this is, they need to see that since they believe in both the six-day creation and Jesus' deity, the only consistent course for them to follow is to show their faith by keeping the Sabbath of creation and creation's Lord.

He who remembers the Sabbath as Christ directs will not forget the Lord. In union with the Creator-Redeemer, he will have no other gods before the Lord. If he truly obeys the fourth commandment in its inner spiritual aspects, he will adhere to the other nine.

Sabbathkeeping distinguishes the true worship of the only true God. Conversely, the substitution by man of any other day in the place of the seventh day marks a false worship in respect to the day so chosen. This is where the line will be drawn in the final conflict between truth and error as portrayed in Revelation 13 and 14.

Christ's authority to command obedience from all is based on His incomparable standing as Lord and Creator of all. His Sabbath points to Him as the Creator-God, thus signifying His authority. If Adam and Eve had fully committed themselves to His authority, they would not have disobeyed Him. Every Christian needs to fully submit himself to Christ's authority, and hallowing His Sabbath demonstrates that submission.

Sunday worship was established among Christians as a substitute for Sabbath worship when men attempted to combine certain pagan elements with Christianity. This unholy union resulted in the establishment of an apostate religious system that dominated Christendom until the Reformation, when its supremacy was broken to some extent.

Do you know that a prominent Baptist minister admitted all this? Dr. E. T. Hiscox, the Baptist preacher who wrote *The Baptist Manual,* in an address to the Baptist ministers of New York State in conference, on November 13, 1893, stated, "Of course, I quite well know that Sunday did come into use in early Christian history as a religious day. . . . But what a pity that it *comes branded with the mark of paganism, and christened with the name of the sun god, when adopted and sanctioned by the papal apostasy,* and *bequeathed as a sacred legacy to Protestantism!"* (Italics supplied.) Such an unsavory origin should lead every Christian to repudiate Sunday-keeping and observe the Bible Sabbath.

All these considerations reveal what an important link the true Sabbath is in the chain of truth as it is in Jesus. How skillfully the all-wise Creator designed the Sabbath! It stands as an effective barrier against many errors, allowing no materialism or humanism which leaves God out of its reckoning; no false theory of evolution substituting its dictums for the truths of God's Word; no legalists attempting to save themselves by their good works, or antinomians advocating that faith in Christ frees a Christian from the obligation to obey the moral laws of the Decalogue.

Such is the power of the Sabbath. Ellen G. White wrote that in the testing times ahead, God's people "will find their power in the sign spoken of in Exodus 31:12-18."—*Selected Messages,* Book Two, p. 55.

The sign of Exodus 31:12-18 is the Sabbath, the sign of Christ the Creator and Sanctifier. Since God's people will find their power in the Sabbath, isn't it plain that they should now present it everywhere as the sign of their Redeemer-Creator? Doesn't this call upon every Christian to enter the Sabbath fortress and abide in safety?

5

THE TEXT THAT NOBODY HAS FOUND

One of the czars of Russia while walking in his park came upon a sentry standing guard over a little patch of weeds. "What are you doing here?" he asked.

The sentry replied, "I don't know. All I know is that the captain of the guard ordered me to stand over this spot."

The czar sent for the captain. "Captain, what is this man guarding?"

The captain answered, "All I know is that the regulations call for a sentry to be posted here."

The czar then ordered an investigation, but no one in the government of Russia could discover why that spot needed guarding. Then they opened the archives, and the mystery was solved. The records showed that a hundred years before, Catherine the Great had planted a rosebush on that plot of ground and ordered a sentry posted there to keep people from trampling on it. Eventually the rosebush died, but nobody thought to cancel the order. And for a hundred years men stood guard over a spot where a rosebush once had grown and didn't know what they were guarding.

Every Christian will do well to open the archives of God's Word and check on the religious plantings he follows. Many Christians adhere to certain practices they think are Biblical but are not.

For example, take the practice of Sunday-keeping. For centuries most Christians have worshiped on Sunday. Thus many have concluded that the New Testament teaches that Christians should keep the first day of the week.

Now, the New Testament mentions the first day of the week eight times—in Matthew 28:1; Mark 16:1, 2, 9; Luke 24:1; John 20:1, 19; Acts 20:7; 1 Corinthians 16:2. If there is Scriptural authority for keeping the first day, it will be found in connection with these eight texts. Let us examine each of them.

First, in Mark 16:9 (N.E.B.) we read, "When he had risen from the dead early on Sunday morning he appeared first to Mary of Magdala, from whom he had formerly cast out seven devils."

This definitely states that Christ arose early on Sunday morning, but nowhere does it hint that the Christian is to honor Sunday because the Lord arose on that day.

Second, in Mark 16:1, 2 (N.E.B.) we find this: "When the Sabbath was over, Mary of Magdala, Mary the mother of James, and Salome bought aromatic oils intending to go and anoint him; and very early on the Sunday morning, just after sunrise, they came to the tomb."

This scripture says that the Sabbath was past when these women came to the tomb at sunrise on Sunday. Regardless of how earnestly people may try, it is impossible to keep the Sabbath on Sunday. Why? Because the Word of God shows that the Sabbath was past before Sunday began. Mark 16: 1, 2 mentions the Sabbath, or Saturday, and the first day, or Sunday, side by side and reveals that the seventh day *is* the Sabbath and the first day *is not* the Sabbath. Third, Matthew 28:1 (N.E.B.) repeats the same point: "The Sabbath had passed, and it was about daybreak on Sunday, when Mary of Magdala and the other Mary came to look at the grave."

Instead of these three texts presenting any evidence for Sunday-keeping, they prove the opposite. They reveal that the Lord's holy day for man is the day preceding Sunday, the day we call Saturday.

Fourth, Luke 23:54-56; 24:1 (N.E.B.) further confirms this: "It was Friday, and the Sabbath was about to begin. The women who had accompanied him from Galilee followed; they took note of the tomb and observed how his body was laid. Then they went home and prepared spices and perfumes; and on the Sabbath they rested in obedience to the commandment. But on the Sunday morning very early they came to the tomb bringing the spices they had prepared."

Notice three facts in these verses:

1. Christ was crucified on Friday, the day before Sabbath. Mark 15:42 designates the day of the crucifixion as the day before the Sabbath.

2. Christ arose from the dead on Sunday, the day after the Sabbath. Mark 16:1, 2 says that the Sabbath was past when the women found the tomb empty.

3. Luke 23:56 indicates that these followers of Jesus kept the Sabbath according to God's commandment on the day *after* the crucifixion and *preceding* the Lord's resurrection. You know that Saturday comes between Friday and Sunday. Luke 23:54-56; 24:1; Mark 16:1, 2; and Matthew 28:1 assure us that the seventh-day Sabbath, or Saturday, is the day which the Lord wants us to keep.

Some wonder, Haven't there been mistakes in the reckoning of the days during these thousands of years since creation? The calendar has been changed several times. How, then, can you be sure that Saturday is the seventh day as specified in the Ten Commandments?

Four facts settle the matter:

1. The calendar changes have pertained to the number of days in a given month. They did not change the fixed order of the days in the weekly cycle. Hence, Saturday is the seventh day, the last day of the week, as it always has been.

2. The Sabbath of God's commandment came in between crucifixion Friday and resurrection Sunday.

3. Luke 23:54-56; 24:1 shows that the followers of Jesus came to the tomb on Sunday to do what they would not do on Sabbath.

4. God's commandment required these followers of Jesus to observe the Sabbath from what we call Friday sunset to Saturday sunset on *the day after the Jewish age ended at the cross*. Hence, it requires the same of us today.

A young member of a large Sunday-keeping denomination began to keep the seventh-day Sabbath as a result of studying the Bible. One day one of the ministers of his church said to him, "Brother _____, you had better go slow on how you take up with this Saturday-Sabbath. There have been so many changes in the calendar that no one can be sure what day the Ten Commandments mention."

The young man asked him, "Reverend _____, are you sure that Sunday is the day on which Christ arose?"

The minister replied, "We are absolutely sure of this."

Then the young man said, "Mark 16:9 declares that Christ arose on the first day of the week. Now, since you are so sure that Sunday is the first day of the week, I can count the days from Sunday as two, three, four, five, six, and seven and be equally sure that the seventh day is Saturday."

The minister, realizing he had been proved wrong by his own statements, turned and left.

The fifth mention of the first day of the week in the New Testament is John 20:1 (N.E.B.): "Early on the Sunday morning, while it was still dark, Mary of Magdala came to the tomb."

Here again there is no mention of Sunday worship. However, the Bible indicates that in the days of the apostles, Christians kept the seventh day and not Sunday. Acts 18:4 reveals that Paul reasoned in the synagogue every Sabbath at Corinth and persuaded the Jews and the Greeks. He did this about A.D. 54, or twenty-three years after Christ's resurrection. Every week the Jews assembled in their synagogues, as was their custom, upon the Sabbath. The Holy Spirit, speaking through Luke, identifies their meeting days as the "Sabbath," still the only Sabbath some twenty years after the resurrection of Christ.

Next, the sixth instance where the New Testament mentions the first day of the week: "Late that Sunday evening, when the disciples were together behind locked doors, for fear of the Jews, Jesus came and stood among them. 'Peace be with you!' he said, and then showed them his hands and his side." John 20:19, N.E.B.

Sometime after sunset on the Sunday of Christ's resurrection, the apostles huddled together in their common abode because they feared for their lives. And Jesus appeared to them. Some claim that the disciples had gathered to inaugurate the keeping of Sunday in honor of Christ's resurrection, but notice that not a word in the text indicates such. In fact, the record shows that they did not believe He had arisen from the dead. (Mark 16:9-14.)

It is dangerous to read into any scripture something different from what it says. "Add thou not unto his words, lest he reprove thee, and thou be found a liar." Proverbs 30:6.

Others will reply, The record does show that the Lord appeared to the disciples on Sunday. So He did. It was His first opportunity to meet with all of them at one time after His resurrection. The record also reveals that He met with them on other days besides Sunday. (See John 21:1-14.)

In John 20:26 the apostle records that after eight days from this previous late Sunday night meeting, Jesus appeared again to His apostles. Some declare that this second meeting took place on the next Sunday and claim that it marked the setting apart of Sunday as a day for worship. But the text does not even hint of such a purpose. Jesus appeared to convince doubting Thomas.

The first Christian Council convened at Jerusalem about A.D. 52, or twenty-one years after Christ's resurrection (see Acts 15), and the decision of this council recognized the seventh day as the only Sabbath. James referred to the regular meeting days when the Jews met in their synagogues as "every *sabbath* day." (Acts 15:21.) The early Christians knew of no Sabbath other than the seventh day of the week.

Notice the seventh instance where the New Testament mentions the first day of the week:

"And upon the first day of the week, when the disciples came together to break bread, Paul preached unto them, ready to depart on the morrow; and continued his speech until midnight." Acts 20:7.

Many claim this shows that Christians regularly met every Sunday for worship. Again we must heed the caution: Don't read into the Scriptures something that isn't there.

In the Bible record the day of twenty-four hours is measured from sunset to sunset. (Genesis 1:19; Mark 1:32.) The first day of the week under this method extends from sunset Saturday to sunset Sunday. It is evident then that this all-night first-day meeting at Troas convened on Saturday night. In addition, this first-day meeting does not represent regular Christian practice, for it lasted all night long. (Acts 20:11.) No church ordinarily holds regular meetings during the entire night.

The Christians met not because it was Sunday but because Paul was "ready to depart" (Acts 20:7), and he went on foot Sunday morning to join his fellow workers at Assos. (Acts 20:13, 14.) It was most logical that the believers at Troas would hold a farewell meeting on Saturday night.

"But," some will rejoin, "the record shows that the disciples broke bread, celebrated the Lord's Supper, on Sunday." Even if we grant that "breaking bread" refers to the Lord's Supper, the Scriptures assert that they did this every day of the week. (Acts 2:46.)

Holding a regular meeting on Sunday, as do the vast majority of Christians, does not make it the divinely appointed weekly holy day. According to Genesis 2:3 and Exodus 20:8-11, the Lord must first rest upon it, then sanctify it, and finally command its observance. And this holds true of no other day of the week except the seventh day.

What does the Book of Acts say about the Sabbath in the years which followed Christ's resurrection? In seven places it identifies the Sabbath as the day when the Jews met for their regular weekly worship (Acts 13:14, 27, 42, 44; 15:21; 17:1, 2; 18:4), thus completely ruling out that the first day, or Sunday, was the Lord's holy day on which His people worshiped in the days of the apostles. Three Christian leaders—Paul, James, and Luke—*designated the successive Saturdays when the Jews assembled for worship as "every sabbath day," or the only Sabbath recognized by Christians in the days of the apostles.* (Acts 13:27; 15:21; 18:4.)

1 Corinthians 16:2 is the eighth instance where the New Testament mentions the first day of the week: "Upon the first day of the week let every one of you lay by him in store,

as God hath prospered him, that there be no gatherings when I come."

Some contend this means that Paul counseled the Corinthians to take a collection every Sunday at church. Therefore, they conclude, Sunday was the regular meeting day. But the text does not say anything to this effect. In fact, Paul advocates just the opposite of a collection at church. "Let every one of you lay by *him in store*." Paul counsels them to lay aside the money at home. The Portuguese, Spanish, and Italian versions of the Bible, as well as certain English versions, render the phrase "lay by at home."

Paul was gathering funds to help the needy saints at Jerusalem and planned to stop at Corinth. He advised them to lay aside some money at home on the first day of each week for this relief fund. Then when he arrived at Corinth, they could turn the money over to him, and he would carry it with him to the needy saints at Jerusalem.

Others reason that Revelation 1:10 calls the first day of the week the Lord's day. John says, "I was in the Spirit on the Lord's day." However, this text does not mention the first day of the week. Therefore, we must let the testimony of the Bible elsewhere decide which day is the Lord's day.

What are the facts? Nowhere in the Bible does the Lord claim the first day as His day, but from the beginning of the world, throughout all the Word of God, the Lord sets forth the seventh day as His sanctified day for mankind. In Isaiah 58:13 the Lord specifically calls the Sabbath "my holy day." Christ claimed to be Lord of the Sabbath, so it is truly the Lord's day. (Mark 2:28.) He made the seventh day His day for man to observe, when He, as the Creator, sanctified it for man.

It is customary among some Christian groups to refer to the seventh day as the Sabbath and Sunday as the Lord's day, but such a distinction is unwarranted according to the

Word of God, for the terms "Sabbath" and "Lord's day" both apply to the seventh day.

Christ's work as Creator in a very special sense makes the seventh day His day—the Lord's day. So it was only natural for John in Revelation 1:10 to call the Sabbath "the Lord's day."

We have examined all the texts which mention the first day of the week, and it is evident that they do not authorize Sunday observance. Since the Lord always has plainly indicated how He wants His people to worship Him and what they should do in religious matters, He surely would have plainly stated that He had discontinued the observance of the seventh day after His crucifixion and had ordained the observance of Sunday if such were the case. But Christ nowhere delineates such a change. Instead, Christ instituted the Lord's Supper and Christian baptism as new ordinances for the Christian age. The record plainly tells how they were instituted. The Bible clearly commands their observance.

The more you read the Bible through, the more you will be convinced of the lack of Biblical evidence for Sunday-keeping.

1. Jesus Christ and His apostles never changed the Sabbath from the seventh day to the first day of the week.

2. Jesus Christ and the apostles never observed the first day of the week for the Sabbath.

3. The New Testament records no divine command to keep the first day of the week.

4. Scripture gives no indication that the first day is to be kept for any reason.

5. The Scriptures nowhere indicate that keeping the first day of the week replaced keeping the seventh day of the week during Bible times.

6. Neither God, Christ, the angels, nor inspired men have said one word in favor of Sunday as a holy day.

In direct contrast, Christ plainly commands the observance of the seventh day in the Decalogue. (Exodus 20: 8-11.) He inseparably connects it with accepting Him as the Creator (Exodus 31:16, 17), the Saviour (Ezekiel 20:12), and the Lord (Ezekiel 20:20). Christ made its observance one of His steps for us to follow. (Luke 4:16; 1 Peter 2:21.) All the saved will honor it forever. (Isaiah 66:22, 23.)

An evangelistic campaign in progress had reached the night when the evangelist would present what the Bible says concerning the Sabbath. "If you folks will read the New Testament through," he asserted, "you will know for yourselves that there is no text which directs us to keep Sunday."

Taking the evangelist's statement to heart, one lady returned home determined to read the New Testament through without delay. She began with Matthew and read on all during the night. She kept on during the next day until she reached the "Amen" at the close of Revelation. Then she announced, "I always thought there was a text somewhere directing Christians to keep Sunday in honor of our Lord's resurrection. Now I know that there isn't any such text. Also I know what to do. From now on I will, by the help of God, keep the seventh day." And she remained faithful to her promise until she died. What if every honest-hearted Sunday-keeper, confronted with the issues involved, would read the Bible through in this manner? Thousands would decide to keep God's Sabbath. When a Christian who keeps Sunday finds no Bible authority for doing so, the only right course for him is to keep the seventh day as the Bible commands.

In the time of Christ some set aside their obligation to care for their fathers and mothers as demanded by the fifth commandment by adhering to a rule of their own devising. How serious did Jesus regard this? He told them, "Ye reject the commandment of God, that ye may keep your own tradition." "Thus have ye made the commandment of God of none effect by your tradition." "In vain do they worship me, teaching for doctrines the commandments of men." (Mark 7:9; Matthew 15:6; Mark 7:7.)

So it is today regarding the fourth commandment. Christians are nullifying this command of God by keeping the first day of the week. According to Jesus, they worship Him in vain when they thus knowingly substitute a man-made day of worship for His true Sabbath. Surely this suffices to cause every Christian to turn from keeping Sunday to observing the true Sabbath of Christ.

Jesus says, "Every plant, which my heavenly Father hath not planted, shall be rooted up." Matthew 15:13. God never planted Sunday-keeping. Is it wise or safe to cling to something that He will root out? Many will go out with it. However, at the close of creation God did plant the keeping of the seventh day, and He will never root it out. It will be honored forever in the new earth.

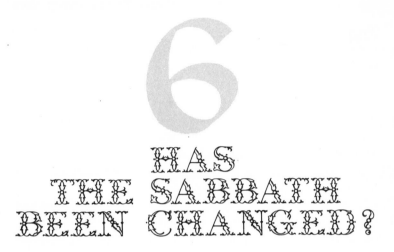

HAS THE SABBATH BEEN CHANGED?

Your birthday commemorates your entrance into this world. Similarly the Sabbath commemorates God's finished work of creating our world in six days and His rest on the seventh day.

Can a person change his birthday from the day of the month on which he was born to another day? "Impossible," you say. Suppose he was born March 7. He might assert that he was born March 1, but that wouldn't change his birthday from March 7. Even if the government passed a resolution stating he had been born March 1, this wouldn't change his real birthday from March 7. He might succeed in leading everyone to believe that he had been born March 1, but this would not alter his real birthday.

Likewise the seventh-day Sabbath birthday of our world cannot be changed to any other day of the week. Christ never changes. He established the Sabbath for man upon the seventh day, thus demonstrating that He is the Lord, the Creator-God, and the only Saviour. Therefore man cannot change the Sabbath even as Christ cannot be changed from being the Lord and the Creator-Saviour.

We have pointed out from Isaiah 66:22, 23 that the Sabbath will be honored forever in the coming new earth. It is an eternal twofold memorial of Christ's eternal twofold relationship to humanity as Creator-Redeemer. How could it ever be changed or abolished?

Men have changed the practice of the majority so that contrary to God's will they use Sunday as the day for rest instead of Saturday as the Lord has commanded. But Christ's Sabbath is still inseparably connected with the last day of the week, and since God's Ten Commandments require the observance of Saturday as the Sabbath, this change from Saturday to Sunday could not be effected without changing the Ten Commandments. Yet God has expressly forbidden man to attempt to change or discard any of His commandments. "Ye shall not add unto the word which I command you, neither shall ye diminish ought from it, that ye may keep the commandments of the Lord your God which I command you." Deuteronomy 4:2. No man, no group of men, have any right to tamper with any of God's commandments.

The Lord spoke the Ten Commandments at Sinai. With His own lips He proclaimed, "The seventh day is the sabbath of the Lord." Further, God declares that He will not alter the thing that is gone out of His lips. (Psalm 89:34.) Surely, then, neither the Father nor the Son has changed the Sabbath from Saturday to Sunday, because they were united in proclaiming the Decalogue at Sinai.

In His Sermon on the Mount Jesus declared that not even the smallest change would be made in the law. "Till heaven and earth pass, one jot or one tittle shall in no wise pass from the law, till all be fulfilled." (Matthew 5:17, 18.)

A jot corresponds to the smallest character in the Hebrew alphabet *(yod)*. A tittle is even smaller—the point of a letter corresponding to the dot on the *i* or the cross on the *t*. Christ taught that the Ten Commandments cannot be changed in the smallest item as long as heaven and earth stand. Obviously Christ did not change the Sabbath from the seventh day to the first.

Christ, in prophesying of the destruction of Jerusalem, which came to pass some thirty-nine years later (A.D. 70), said, "But pray ye that your flight be not in the winter, neither on the sabbath day." Matthew 24:20. Jesus thus indicated that the same seventh-day Sabbath that His disciples observed before His death would still be the Sabbath of the Lord in A.D. 70—thirty-nine years after His resurrection.

"If the keeping of the seventh day is binding on Christians," some may ask, "why then is there no command concerning it in the New Testament?"

The New Testament mentions the Sabbath over fifty times, and nowhere does it reject the Sabbath of the Old Testament or recommend any other day in its place. Both Testaments exemplify the unity of all truth in Christ by teaching the same Saviour, the same gospel, the same Ten Commandments, and the same Sabbath.

Still others insist, "All the Ten Commandments are repeated in the New Testament except the Sabbath commandment, showing that keeping the seventh day is not binding on Christians."

However, they argue from a false premise. Only a few of the Ten Commandments are repeated verbatim in the New Testament. Does this mean that the others are not binding? Not at all. The New Testament writers did not need to repeat or reenact them all to make them binding, because none of them ever were repealed. None expired by limitation. Hence, all of them, including the Sabbath command, remain in force as long as right is right. However, three apostles—Paul, James, and John—in their epistles refer to the Ten Commandments as the standard of righteousness for Christians. (Romans 3:31; 7:7; 13:8-10; Ephesians 6:2; James 2:8-12; 1 John 3:4; 2:3, 4.)

Many Christians believe that the apostles originated the custom of keeping Sunday in the place of the seventh day. But God's Word in the Acts of the Apostles demonstrates that the apostles regarded the seventh day as the only weekly holy day for the Lord's people.

Eight statements in the Book of Acts refer to the Sabbath day. (Acts 13:14, 27, 42, 44; 15:21; 16:13; 17:1-3; 18:4.) The Holy Spirit speaking through Luke, who wrote Acts, could not have called the seventh day *the* Sabbath day in the decades following Christ's crucifixion if, as some claim, the Sabbath was abolished at the cross or if the keeping of the first day had replaced observance of the seventh day among Christians. These eight references constitute an eightfold proof that the apostles did not change the Sabbath.

Neander, one of the greatest church historians, says that the apostles did not intend to transfer the Sabbath laws to Sunday. In his book *The History of the Christian Religion and Church* he wrote:

"The festival of Sunday, like all other festivals, *was only a human ordinance,* and it was far from the intentions of the apostles . . . and from the early apostolic Church, to transfer the laws of the Sabbath to Sunday." (John Henry Rose's translation, p. 186. Italics supplied.)

Seven of these references in the Book of Acts speak of the Sabbath in connection with the weekly worship day of the Jews at their synagogues. Everybody knows that the Jews customarily assembled at the synagogue for worship on the seventh day of the week. Hence, these seven references stand as witnesses that the day we call Saturday was the Christian Sabbath.

Some attempt to offset this by suggesting that Paul went to the Jewish synagogue on Sabbath in order to preach Christ, but this doesn't change the fact that the Holy Spirit, in speaking through Luke, does not refer to the seventh day as the Jewish Sabbath or the former Sabbath but as *the* Sabbath day.

Since the transfer of worship on the seventh day to the first day did not occur in New Testament times, it must have been effected *by uninspired men after the New Testament was written.* Thus the change rests solely on the authority of man without the authority of Scripture.

We could cite many statements from Protestants in which they freely admit that there is no Bible authority for the observance of the first day of the week. We shall cite only one.

"And where are we told in Scripture that we are to keep the first day at all? We are commanded to keep the seventh; but we are nowhere commanded to keep the first day. . . . The reason why we keep the first day of the week holy instead of the seventh is for the same reason that we observe many other things, not because the Bible, but because the church, has enjoined it."—Rev. Isaac Williams, B.D. (Church of England), *Plain Sermons on the Catechism,* Vol. 1, pp. 334-336.

You ask, "When did this change take place?" It took place during the second, third, fourth, and fifth centuries. Many Christians worshiped on both Saturday and Sunday for several generations. Throughout the ages a faithful group has kept the seventh day.

How was it changed? Among the many factors solidifying the change were two significant events. On March 7,

A.D. 321, Constantine, Emperor of Rome, signed the first law requiring people to rest on Sunday. Several decades later a church council at Laodicea decreed that Christians should henceforth cease resting on the seventh day and should rest on the first day of the week instead.

Eusebius, an eminent bishop in the Church in the days of Emperor Constantine, wrote:

"All things whatsoever that it was duty to do on the Sabbath, those *we* [the church] have transferred to the Lord's day [Sunday]."—*Commentary on the Psalms,* Column 1172 in Vol. 23 of Migne's *Patrologia Graeca.*

Notice that he doesn't say Jesus changed the Sabbath. He doesn't say the apostles changed it. When he says, "All things whatsoever that it was duty to do on the Sabbath, those *we have transferred to the Lord's day,*" by "we" he refers to the Church, in which he served as bishop.

Bible prophecy foretold a great falling away from the truth among the professed followers of Christ in post-apostolic times. It foretold that an apostate religious system would rule over Western Europe for many centuries after the fall of the Roman Empire in the West. The supremacy of the ecclesiastical empire of Rome, the Papacy, fulfilled this prophecy.

Daniel 7:25 foretold that this power would think to change the law and times of God. The basic measurement of time is the week, as outlined in the Sabbath command. Changing the times and the law points to an attempt to change God's Sabbath commandment. The Catholic power freely recognizes that they changed the Sabbath from Saturday to Sunday.

In Peter Geiermann's *Convert's Catechism of Catholic Doctrine* (1957 edition), page 50, we read:

"*Q. Which is the Sabbath day?*

"*A.* Saturday is the Sabbath day.

"Q. Why do we observe Sunday instead of Saturday?

"A. We observe Sunday instead of Saturday because the Catholic Church *transferred the solemnity from Saturday to Sunday."* (Emphasis supplied.)

The Catholic Encyclopedia says:

"The [Catholic] Church, . . . after changing the day of rest from the Jewish Sabbath, or seventh day of the week, to the first, made the Third Commandment refer to Sunday as the day to be kept holy as the Lord's Day."—Vol. 4, p. 153.

Additional citations could be set forth, but these two suffice to show that the Roman Catholic power admits that it changed the Sabbath from Saturday to Sunday.

Dr. Nicholas Summerbell, one of the founding fathers of the Disciples of Christ, or the Christian denomination, wrote a *History of the Christian Church.* On page 415, in speaking of the Roman Catholic Church, he says, "It has reversed the Fourth Commandment by doing away with the Sabbath of God's word, and instituting Sunday as a holiday."

Some have asked, Doesn't history show that the Christians regarded Sunday as sacred before there was a Roman Catholic Church? How then can the transfer of the day of rest from Saturday to Sunday be attributed to the Catholic power?

It is true that soon after the apostles passed away, some Christians attached special significance to Sunday, but history discloses that the official sanction for substituting Sunday for the Sabbath was, in general, established under the rule of the Roman Catholic power.

Father Brady, a Catholic priest, delivered an address at Elizabeth, New Jersey, on March 17, 1903. The Elizabeth, New Jersey, *News* of March 18, 1903, reported it: "It is well to remind the Presbyterians, Baptists, Methodists, and all other Christians, that the Bible does not support them anywhere in their observance of Sunday. . . . Sunday is an institution of the Roman Catholic church, and those who observe the day observe a commandment of the Catholic church."

Catholics have recognized that the Sabbath issue is the key to being a true Protestant. *The Catholic Mirror* of December 23, 1893, said, "Reason and common sense demand the acceptance of one or the other of these alternatives: either Protestantism and the keeping holy of Saturday, or Catholicity and the keeping holy of Sunday. Compromise is impossible."

All must respond to the question, What will you do about it? May each decide, "I will not bow to the directions of human beings. By the grace of God, I purpose to walk according to the commandments of the Lord. I want His Sabbath in my life as the sign that He is my Creator-Redeemer." With the resoluteness of Martin Luther may each of us say, "Here I take my stand, God helping me. I can do no other."

7

DOES IT MAKE ANY DIFFERENCE?

Mr. Lord, who lived in the seventh and last house on a dead-end street, invited his friends in the city to attend his birthday celebration. Each invitation bore the directions to his place: "Turn right from Main Street onto Week Street and come to the seventh and last house."

If you read such directions, would you stop at the first house to meet Mr. Lord? No. You would not expect to meet him at any of the first six houses. You would pass the first six houses and approach the seventh, saying, "This is the place. Here is where the birthday celebration will be held."

So it is with the Lord of all and the birthday celebration of the creation of this world. The Sabbath forms the meeting place and connecting link between this blessed Creator-Redeemer and man.

In Exodus 20:8-11 He commands every soul to hallow

the seventh day because He made the world in six days, rested on the seventh day, and sanctified it, or set it apart. Each succeeding last day of the week was for man to observe. Thus, when the Lord directs us to hallow the seventh day, He does not mean any day in the seven. He makes it very plain that His Sabbath is *the same day of the week on which He, as the Creator-God, rested after He had made the world in six days. Therefore, it cannot apply to any other day except the last day of the week—the seventh day.*

God's Word, in Luke 23:54 to 24:1, confirms that the Sabbath according to the Lord's commandment is the seventh day of the week—the day between the Friday of the crucifixion and the Sunday of the resurrection.

The Sabbath is not merely a day of physical rest. Any day would do for that. Neither is it merely a day for spiritual renewal. It is both, yet even more. It is the sign of Christ our Creator-Saviour. No other day aside from the seventh can acceptably substitute.

We disobey our Lord Jesus Christ when we neglect to keep the seventh day as He commands and substitute another day in its place, and the difference between obedience and disobedience to Jesus is the infinite difference between going to heaven or being cast into the lake of fire.

Make no mistake about it. The Sabbath-versus-Sunday controversy is not merely a question as to whether we shall rest on Saturday or Sunday. *The basic issue involves obedience to Christ.* It is a question of, Whom shall we obey as supreme? Shall we have another god before the Lord? Shall we obey the Lord and keep the seventh day as He has commanded, or shall we obey custom and human tradition which enjoin us to keep Sunday?

When a Christian encounters such an issue, his love for Christ leads him to obey his Lord and observe His Sabbath, for the only right way is to always obey Christ.

Millions like to think the observance of Sunday is right under present-day circumstances, but it is a fatal mistake to decide which day to keep on the basis of personal preference. Proverbs 16:25 describes the inadequacy of deciding one's course by personal inclination. The way seems right but ends in destruction.

Six thousand years of misery and suffering have devolved on humanity because Adam and Eve accepted the devil's suggestion that it didn't make any difference whether or not they ate the fruit from the Lord's reserved tree. We would do well to respect the seventh day which the Lord has reserved as His holy day. God has dealt decidedly with the inadequacy of following personal inclination. "Ye shall *not* do . . . every man whatsoever is right in his own eyes." Deuteronomy 12:8.

Some may ask, If I am not to do what I think is right, what shall I do? The Lord replies, "Observe . . . all these words which I command thee, that it may go well with thee, . . . *when thou doest that which is good and right in the sight of the Lord thy God*." Verse 28.

The only recourse is to do what is right in God's sight, according to His law, and those who truly keep the seventh day are doing what is right in His sight. Those who fail to keep it are not doing what is right in His sight in this respect. How is it with you?

Can you, or any other person, make a day holy? No. We can keep holy only that which God has previously made holy. Since the seventh day is the only day in the week the Lord ever made holy, it is the only day we can keep holy. Christ first hallowed the Sabbath, so we by His grace may honor it.

When the heathen assert, "It makes no difference what god I worship, just so long as I worship a god," every Christian quickly replies, "There is only one true God, the

Creator. To worship any other god is disobedience to His first commandment. It is wrong and useless."

The same holds true for the Christian who says, "It makes no difference what day I keep, just as long as I rest one day in seven." There is only one true Sabbath—the last day of the week. When we set it aside, keeping any other day, we disobey God's Sabbath commandment, and such worship is wrong and useless. Thus Jesus said, "But in vain they do worship me, teaching for doctrines the commandments of men." Matthew 15:9.

Others may ask, Didn't Paul say in Colossians 2:16, 17 that the Sabbath of the Jewish regime was not to be imposed upon Christians? Let us consider this scripture. "Let no man therefore judge you in meat, or in drink, or in respect of an holyday, or of the new moon, or of the sabbath days: which are a shadow of things to come; but the body is of Christ."

The Bible, when rightly interpreted, never contradicts itself. Those who interpret Colossians 2:16, 17 to mean that Christ abolished the seventh-day Sabbath at the cross have the wrong interpretation. Why? Because they make Colossians contradict those eight places in the Book of Acts which relate the observance of the "sabbath day" in the decades after the crucifixion. Also they make it contradict all those other texts which declare that the Ten Commandments are a binding code after the cross.

The word *Sabbath,* a transliteration of the Hebrew word *shabbath,* signifies "rest." The Hebrew cognate verb *shabbath* means "to cease, to rest, or to keep a sabbath." The verb is used twice in Genesis 2:2, 3, where it is translated "rested," indicating that Christ's rest on the seventh day at the close of His creative work made the seventh day the Sabbath in the beginning. In Exodus 20:11 the Lord refers to the seventh day as the Sabbath in the beginning before sin entered. This shows that the weekly Sabbath is excluded from those typical yearly sabbaths and ceremonial observances which were instituted much later and which were abolished at the cross.

But doesn't Paul in Romans 14:5, 6 sanction the keeping of any day a person may choose? Let us read what he says:

"One man esteemeth one day above another: another esteemeth every day alike. Let every man be fully persuaded in his own mind. He that regardeth the day, regardeth it unto the Lord; and he that regardeth not the day, to the Lord he doth not regard it."

Does this mean that Christians need not keep any fixed day in the week? Is Paul sanctioning the keeping of any day that a person may choose? Not at all. Why not? Because this interpretation would make Romans 14:5, 6 contradict Christ's Sabbath command in Exodus 20:8-11. Also it would make Paul contradict his own teachings that Christians must obey the Ten Commandments. (Ephesians 6:2; Romans 7:7; 3:31; 13:8-10.)

If we take into account the existing situation in the church at Rome, the passage becomes clear. This church, as well as churches in some other cities, was composed in part of Jews who had accepted Christ and in part of some Gentiles who had become Christians.

These Jewish Christians from their childhood had observed various yearly holy days of the ceremonial law, such as the Passover, Pentecost, the Day of Atonement, etc., which were no longer binding after the cross, as we have pointed out previously. No one needed to honor them after Jesus died on the cross, but many of these Jewish Christians continued to observe them.

The Gentile believers had no background of experience in these ceremonial holy days and ignored them. Thus, dissension arose in the church. The Jewish believers found fault with the Gentile converts because they had no regard for the

Passover, Pentecost, the Day of Atonement, etc. The Gentile believers criticized the Jewish Christians because they continued to observe these yearly holy days that had been fulfilled by Christ's death on the cross. Paul gave this counsel to alleviate this dispute.

To the Jewish believers he said, "If you wish to observe these days of the ceremonial law, do so, but do not judge your Gentile brother in Christ who ignores them."

To the Gentile Christians he wrote, "If you know that these are abolished and therefore ignore them, don't judge your Jewish brethren who continue to observe them."

In short—"Let us not judge one another." This is the main point in Romans 14.

When we understand that Romans 14:5, 6 referred to Jewish national holidays and not to the seventh-day Sabbath of the Ten Commandments, then this text harmonizes with all the rest of the Bible concerning the Sabbath.

Dr. Raoul Dederen has written: "Who can have a divine commandment before him and say to others: you can treat that commandment as you please; it really makes no difference whether you keep it or not; please yourselves? No apostle could so conduct an argument. And probably no man would be more surprised at that interpretation than Paul himself, who had utmost respect for the Decalogue, God's law, which is 'holy, just and good' (Rom. 7:12). For the apostle each of the ten commandments is an expression of love (ch. 13:8-10), and Christ himself, the norm of all Pauline teaching (see, for instance, ch. 15:1-13), was indisputably a Sabbath keeper."—"On Esteeming One Day Better Than Another," *Andrews University Seminary Studies,* Vol. IX, No. 1, January, 1971, pp. 27, 28.

The Sabbath is enshrined among the eternal sanctities of Christ's Ten Commandments. The harmony of truth in Him establishes that nothing in the New Testament, when rightly interpreted, contradicts obedience to the Decalogue with its command to observe the seventh-day Sabbath. The Christian cannot ignore the Sabbath any more than he can ignore the other nine precepts.

The use of the seven-day week among nearly all nations testifies to the continuity of the Sabbath and also indicates that it is a specific day—the last day of the week. The origin of the septenary cycle of time is bound together with the origin of the Sabbath, and it cannot be accounted for from nature.

The rotation of the earth upon its axis in twenty-four hours determines the length of our day. The revolution of the moon around our planet indicates the months. The revolution of the earth around the sun in a little over 365 days marks the year of 365¼ days. But why seven days to a week? Genesis 1 and 2 gives the answer. Christ the Creator made the week when He created the world in six days and rested on the seventh day. He directed man to use six days for his own affairs and to devote the seventh day to the Lord.

The universal use of seven days for a week reveals how the Sabbath has shaped world practice. The Sabbath at the end of each week points to Christ as the Creator-God and bears its own witness that the days of creation were not long periods of time but twenty-four-hour days. Therefore by using the week of seven days, all nations tacitly acknowledge that the seventh day is the Sabbath of the Lord.

A man at Detroit bought a railroad ticket for Grand Rapids, Michigan, but unknowingly boarded a limited eastbound flyer. The train had crossed the Detroit River and proceeded into Canada before the conductor came through. When the traveler handed him his ticket, the conductor said, "Man, you are on the wrong train. Your ticket says 'Grand Rapids,' and here you are in Canada going in the wrong direction."

The man became excited and refused to believe the conductor. He wanted to argue about it because he felt sure he was right. But finally he said to the conductor, "Well, what shall I do?"

"Get off at the first stop, take the next train back to Detroit, and get on the right train for Grand Rapids," the conductor replied.

The man had ridden forty miles thinking he had boarded the right train, but he was going in the wrong direction all the time. "There is a way that seemeth right unto a man, but the end thereof are the ways of death." Proverbs 16:25.

If a man is on the wrong train, he will never reach the right destination no matter how sincere he may be unless he changes to the right train.

God's heaven-bound train runs on the Christ-track of the commandments. Revelation 22:14 says, "Blessed are they that do his commandments, that they may have right to the tree of life, and may enter in through the gates into the city."

RIGHT DAY — WRONG WAY

Serving supper, the housewife passed everyone a piece of cake. As they began eating it, she noticed quizzical looks on their faces, meaning, What is wrong with the cake?

In answer to their questioning glances she said, "I had the right recipe in my hand, but I thought by using more of certain ingredients I would improve the cake. But it turned out wrong."

Similarly some Christians hold to the only right day for the Sabbath—the last day of the week, but they keep it in the wrong way.

Consider how the Pharisees and legalists kept the seventh-day Sabbath in the time of Christ. To God's Sabbath commandment they had added numerous burdensome rules of their own devising. For example: A man was not permitted to use a crutch on the Sabbath, for it involved carrying a burden. If he used a wooden leg, he had to remove it on Sabbath. If one took sick on the Sabbath, he had to wait until sundown before receiving help. They declared that healing cripples and other sick persons on the Sabbath was a sin, but if an ox fell into a pit on the Sabbath, they would work all day to rescue it.

What hypocrites! They had the right day, but kept it in the wrong way. Their senseless and exacting rules made the Sabbath a day of gloom and depression, but Jesus brushed aside these burdensome and unjust Sabbath rules by restoring the Sabbath as a day of joy and blessing.

Some assert, The Bible says that Christ broke the Sabbath, and this shows He intended to abolish it. Such is not true. The Bible doesn't say Christ ever broke the Sabbath. It does record that the Pharisees accused Him of Sabbathbreaking because He restored certain cripples on the Sabbath. (John 9:16.)

Christ broke the Jewish Sabbath regulations, but He kept the Sabbath as required in the Ten Commandments. Sin is the transgression of the law (1 John 3:4), and if Christ had failed to keep the Sabbath according to the Decalogue, He would have been a sinner and could not have saved us from sin. He who charges Christ with Sabbathbreaking voids his own salvation. Since the Bible says He "did no sin" (1 Peter 2:22), we know that He obeyed all the commandments.

In direct contrast to those who swing to the right by exacting man-made restrictions, others swing to the left by professing to keep the Sabbath, but they make it a holiday instead of Christ's holy day. Since they don't have to report for work, they think they are free to use the day for their own pleasures. They hold to the right day in the wrong way.

Still other Christians who profess to observe the seventh day make it merely a day for their own rest and fail to enter

Christ's rest. Christ made the Sabbath primarily as a spiritual rest for man. The word *Sabbath* transliterates the Hebrew word for rest. Hence, the expression in the law—"the seventh day is the sabbath of the Lord"—is equivalent to "the seventh day is the rest of the Lord."

No one can keep the Sabbath as Christ directs unless he first responds to Christ's invitation, "Come unto me, all ye that labour and are heavy laden, and I will give you rest." Matthew 11:28. Unless we enter Christ's rest in keeping the seventh day, we are keeping the right day in the wrong way.

A man may abstain from his work on the seventh day and yet not enter the rest of God. The vast majority of the Israelites and many who today hold to the seventh day have failed here.

A criminal in a cell ten feet square cannot work on Saturday, but this does not mean he is a Sabbathkeeper. No one can keep Christ's Sabbath unless he first allows Christ to dwell in him. If a person who professes to keep the seventh day doesn't have clean hands and a pure heart by the operation of divine grace, he pollutes the Sabbath (Ezekiel 20: 13, 14), and God says that He will pour out His fury on such persons (Ezekiel 20:21).

The Lord asks us to observe the Sabbath as a sign that He sanctifies us. (Exodus 31:13; Ezekiel 20:12.) However, one's keeping of the seventh day cannot truly signify sanctification unless he has been born again and Christ's indwelling presence is sanctifying him every day. A living experience in Christ and His true Sabbath go hand in hand. The right day and a person who doesn't have the right experience in Christ do not fit together. Only he who experiences sanctification in Christ every day can keep Christ's sanctified Sabbath on the last day of the week. Regardless of how carefully he may abstain from work on Saturday, he pollutes the Sabbath unless he has a pure heart and a holy life. God calls us to first of all let Him make us partake of Christ's sanctifying power. Then we can keep the seventh day as an effective sign of Christ as our Creator and Saviour.

The devil does all he can to prevent us from observing the Sabbath because he knows that it effectively links the believer in close fellowship with Christ. Also he realizes that Sabbath observance tests obedience and that he who truly keeps the Sabbath will have committed himself to obey the other commandments. Therefore, he has led millions of Christians to set the true Sabbath aside and to substitute a man-made sabbath in its place. He has led others who hold to the seventh day to observe it very laxly. Thus it means nothing to them because they have no real connection with Christ. He leads yet others to the opposite extreme of burying the Sabbath under their own burdensome restrictions.

Harsh and unreasonable Puritanical rules lead people to look upon God as a hardhearted tyrant rather than a loving heavenly Father. Lax Sabbath observance leads people to regard God as a joking grandfather who will tolerate anything. On the other hand, true Sabbathkeeping constitutes one of the principal means of really knowing God and His true character. "Hallow my sabbaths; and they shall be a sign . . . *that ye may know that I am the Lord.*" Ezekiel 20:20. It is doubtful that one's concept of God is any more accurate than the quality of his Sabbath observance.

True Sabbathkeeping, the sign of Christ as the Creator-Saviour, distinguishes between His way of truth and every false way, between those who worship the true God in His appointed way and countless millions who worship contrary to God's law.

The orthodox Jew observes the Sabbath from Friday sunset to Saturday sunset in memory of creation, but he doesn't understand that the Son of God is this Creator. He has the right day, but he cannot keep it in the right way because he doesn't have Jesus, the Lord of the Sabbath.

Millions of Christians base everything on accepting Christ as Lord and only Saviour, but, by leaving off the observance of the seventh day, they don't acknowledge the appointed sign of their Lord and Saviour.

In the midst of all these well-meaning individuals God has a people who are fully committed to Christ as Lord and Saviour, and they manifest their faith in Him by keeping His Sabbath to signify that Christ is the Creator-Lord and the only Saviour.

Some may still argue, There have been so many changes through all the thousands of years since God set apart the seventh day that no one can be sure our Saturday is the exact day God sanctified. If the Jews had been wrong in their calculations as to the identity of the Sabbath, Jesus would surely have set them right when He lived among them, but He kept the same Sabbath day they did.

The Romans, who ruled Palestine when Jesus lived there, called the seventh day of the week which Jesus observed the day of Saturn (or Saturday). That seventh day which Jesus kept and directs us to keep is identical with the day now known as Saturday.

If you knew which day Jesus would observe if He lived in your town as He once did in Nazareth, wouldn't you happily keep it? Certainly. Has Jesus changed in respect to being the right Way? "Jesus Christ [is] the same yesterday, and to day, and for ever." Hebrews 13:8. Since He has not changed, isn't it plain that if He lived here now, He would keep the same Sabbath that He did when He lived here before? He left us an example that we should follow His steps (1 Peter 2:21), and the observance of the seventh day is one of Christ's steps we should take with Him during each week.

Jesus connected His lordship with the seventh-day Sabbath when He said, "The Son of man is Lord also of the sabbath." Mark 2:28.

Do you accept Jesus as Lord? As surely as you do, you should accept the Sabbath of which He is the Lord, for it is a part of His lordship. The word "also" in this text is significant, because some willingly accept Christ as Lord of all in their life except in Sabbath observance. But we must accept Christ as Lord of all, or He is not our Lord at all.

Christ's proclamation that He is Lord of the Sabbath forever debarred the Pharisees, the disciples, or anyone else from tampering with the Sabbath in any manner. None had any right or ability to transfer its sacredness from the seventh day to any other day. The Sabbath stands solely under Christ's jurisdiction. Man has no control over it whatsoever.

When the heathen substituted their false gods for the only true God, they changed the truth of God into a lie. (Romans 1:21-25.) Likewise when Christians substitute the observance of the first day for the Sabbath of the Lord, they change the truth of God into a lie, even though they are not aware of the consequences.

If every Christian realized what is involved when he sets aside the observance of the seventh day in favor of keeping Sunday, he would not do it, for it means disobedience to the Lord Jesus Christ, setting aside the sign of Christ as the Creator and the only Saviour, and rejecting His authority as the Lawgiver.

"Yes, but," some may say, "this very text [Exodus 31: 16, 17] which speaks of the Sabbath as a sign of creation expressly declares that the Sabbath is a sign between the Lord and the children of Israel. How then can it be a sign to Christians today?"

Doesn't creation pertain to Christians and all Gentiles as much as it does to Jews? None of them would be here without it. Even so the seventh-day Sabbath as a sign of the

Creator and creation pertains to all. Everyone needs to keep it to show his faith in and supreme allegiance to Christ as the Creator of all. Christ forever settled the question when He insisted, "The sabbath was made for man." Mark 2:27. The Sabbath is no more restricted to the Jews than are the other nine precepts of the eternal Ten.

The Bible repeatedly refers to the only true God as the "God of Israel." Does this imply that the true God belongs exclusively to the Jews? Certainly not! He is the only God for every soul. Merely the fact that God's people of old kept the true Sabbath does not preclude its being the only true Sabbath for everyone.

God committed His Word, His Ten Commandments, His Sabbath, and His Son in human form to the Jews because at that time they alone served Him, but this didn't restrict any of these blessings to the Jewish nation. Otherwise Gentiles would have no hope.

Others may insist, The Sabbath is not for Christians because they are not Israelites. This directly contradicts the New Testament, which teaches that the Lord considers all Gentiles and Jews who truly accept Christ as Israelites. (Galatians 3:29; Romans 9:6-8.)

God has inscribed the names of the twelve tribes of Israel over the twelve gates of His eternal city in heaven, the New Jerusalem. (Revelation 21:12.) Hence, Christians will continue to be considered the twelve tribes of spiritual Israel throughout eternity, and in keeping with Exodus 31:16, 17, the Sabbath will forever signify the Creator in the new earth. (Isaiah 66:22, 23.)

When we sum up what the Bible teaches concerning Sabbath observance, five facts stand out in bold relief:

1. The seventh day is the only day of the week that the Lord Jesus Christ as Creator ever sanctified, or set apart, for man.

2. The seventh day is the only day of the week that the Son of God ever blessed for man.

3. The seventh day of the week is the only day of the week that Christ, as the Lord of the Ten Commandments, ever commanded any person to keep.

4. The seventh day is the only day of the week that Christ ever appointed as the sign that He is the Creator-God and only Saviour.

5. The seventh day is the only day of the week which commemorates both creation and redemption in Christ.

These Scriptural considerations show the inseparable connection between keeping the seventh day and obeying the Lord Jesus. What else can a person who accepts Christ do but keep the seventh day, the only day Christ has ever blessed, sanctified, and commanded us to keep? If a person has determined to do what the Lord wants him to do, what else can he do but keep the seventh day as his Lord directs?

But what about all those good Christians who have died keeping the wrong day? Will all who now keep Sunday miss heaven?

God judges everyone according to the light and opportunities he has had for learning and obeying the truth. He will condemn no one for keeping the wrong day through ignorance. (Acts 17:30.) Condemnation comes only when a person willfully refuses to obey the truth.

When we know that Saturday is the right day to keep and refuse or neglect to keep it, He will hold this against us as sin. (James 4:17.) Jesus said, "If ye were blind, ye should have no sin: but now ye say, We see; therefore your sin remaineth." John 9:41.

Every true Christian obeys truth as fast as God's Word points it out. (John 8:47; Luke 8:15.) God's eye is on every honest soul in every country (2 Chronicles 16:9), and He will lead such into His truth.

In order to be ready for heaven, the blood of Jesus Christ and the application of His righteousness must continuously cleanse us from sin, and on this basis we obey the truth as fast as it comes to us from the Bible. "If we walk in the light, . . . the blood of Jesus Christ his Son cleanseth us from all sin." 1 John 1:7. The only course for every sincere, convicted soul is to obey the truth concerning Sabbath observance as it comes to him from the Word of God.

Every person is on probation to test his obedience to God. Each one determines for himself whether or not he will pass the test by his choice to obey or disobey. If he chooses the Lord Jesus as his personal Saviour, then he will allow Christ to live out in him His obedience to God's law. (Galatians 2:20.)

"Ye are my friends, if ye do whatsoever I command you." John 15:14.

"O that there were such an heart in them, that they would fear me, and keep all my commandments always, that it might be well with them, and with their children for ever!" Deuteronomy 5:29.

9

A DOUBLE PORTION FOR YOU

The seventh day bears the distinction of being the only day of the week on which God has placed a special blessing. The Word says, "God blessed the seventh day, and sanctified it: *because* that in it he *had* rested from all his work." Genesis 2:3. God did not limit His blessing to the first Sabbath day only, but He extended it to every Sabbath to follow. He has also pronounced a special blessing on those who keep His Sabbath holy. "Blessed is the man . . . that keepeth the sabbath from polluting it." Isaiah 56:2.

A blessed day and a blessed Person meet in true Sabbathkeeping as Christ's Sabbath brings His double blessing upon the faithful believer. Each one determines the measure of this divine blessing he will receive by how sincerely he meets Christ on His Sabbath. Furthermore, this double blessing is an essential factor in enjoying the best in this life and in being prepared for immortality in God's coming better world.

God not only blessed the seventh day, He also hallowed it with His presence (Exodus 20:11); and having originally hallowed it, He asks us to cooperate with His plan by hallowing it in our lives. The idea that we can keep any day holy is wrong. We can keep holy only the day Christ has made holy, the last day of the week.

A consciousness of the abiding presence of the Lord Jesus is one of life's greatest imperatives. "As a shield from temptation and an inspiration to purity and truth, no other influence can equal the sense of God's presence."—Ellen G. White, *Education,* p. 255.

We should cultivate our consciousness of the presence of Jesus every waking hour of every day, but the Sabbath, the only day He has specially hallowed by His presence, affords a fuller enjoyment of His presence if we make it a meeting place with our Lord. An illustration of this may be drawn when John said, "I was in the Spirit on the Lord's day." Revelation 1:10.

The presence of Jesus provides rest (Exodus 33:14), and true Sabbathkeeping means entering into Christ's rest. (Hebrews 4:4-10.) It is for our own good that in the busy rush of life God calls a halt on the last day of the week and says, "Be still, and know that I am God." Psalm 46:10.

When you truly love God, you know in your inmost soul that all of His commandments are for your good always. (Deuteronomy 6:25.) You see that he who sins against God wrongs his own soul (Proverbs 8:36), and your uppermost desire is to obey Christ, leading to your lasting decision to follow Him all the way to the end. Then you understand that God did not ordain Sabbath observance to deprive you of time for your own activities but to provide time for you to maintain in a special way a closer fellowship with

Him. His Sabbath lifts your eyes from your own things of temporal value so that you can fix them on Christ's things of eternal worth.

We should also note here that Saturday as reckoned by man today does not exactly coincide with the seventh day as reckoned in Scripture. We reckon Saturday from midnight Friday to midnight Saturday. But the Sabbath, according to Christ's command, extends from Friday sunset to Saturday sunset. The Bible rule for computing the day of twenty-four hours is from evening to evening, or from sunset to sunset. (Genesis 1:23, 31; Mark 1:32.)

In Leviticus 23:32 God definitely instructed Israel that they should celebrate the yearly ceremonial sabbath of the Day of Atonement from evening to evening, and the same rule applies for beginning and ending the weekly Sabbath.

In keeping with this rule of the Sabbath beginning at sunset on the sixth day, or Friday, we read that Nehemiah, the governor of Jerusalem, ordered the gates of Jerusalem closed as it began to grow dark before the Sabbath began. (Nehemiah 13:19.)

In the same way we should carefully protect the edges of the Sabbath, and what better way can we do so than by gathering the family for worship at Friday sunset and Sabbath sunset? As we welcome the Sabbath with praise and prayer when it arrives, we set the tempo for a closer fellowship with God by encouraging a spirit of sacred regard for its remaining hours. Then how fitting at sunset on Sabbath to have a special worship of thanksgiving for the blessings of the day and to ask for special help to live rightly during the ensuing week until we greet the next Sabbath at Friday sunset.

The entire period from Friday sunset to Saturday sunset is God's holy time, and if man withholds any part, he is guilty of disobedience and robbery against God.

Those who wait until Saturday morning to begin observing the Sabbath have only a 50 percent Sabbath. No one can keep the Sabbath as God intends unless he begins its observance when it arrives at sunset. If he begins its observance one or two hours after sunset, he is lagging behind the Lord's schedule; but those who go through the gates into the New Jerusalem at the end will not lag behind His schedule.

All business items and secular activities should be laid aside before sunset on the sixth day. The Bible indicates that buying and selling on the Sabbath is wrong. (Nehemiah 13:15-18.) Those who use the Sabbath for their own work and business tread God's Sabbath underfoot, and God appeals to them to stop trampling His Sabbath. (Isaiah 58:13.)

We should withdraw our minds and bodies from worldly business before the Sabbath begins, and we should not allow business discussion or planning to encroach on the Sabbath hours. He who is in a hurry for the sun to set on Saturday evening so that he can resume his business or sports is very much out of line with the spirit of true Sabbathkeeping. (Amos 8:5.)

God is particular how we obey His commandments and demands explicit and implicit obedience. (1 Samuel 15:22; Hebrews 5:9.) Jesus taught that many who perform wonderful works for Him will be denied entrance into heaven because they have disobeyed His commandments. (Matthew 7:21-23.)

He places great importance on the way people observe the Sabbath. God through Jeremiah told the Jews that the fate of Jerusalem depended upon whether they hallowed or polluted the Sabbath. (Jeremiah 17:21-27.) He promised that if they hallowed the Sabbath as He commanded, Jerusalem would stand forever as a spiritual capital for the world, but if they polluted the Sabbath, Jerusalem would be destroyed.

In Isaiah 56:1-4 God connects keeping the Sabbath sacred with keeping the hand from doing any evil and with choosing the things that please Him. In Ezekiel 20:12-21 He interlocks the polluting of the Sabbath with rebellion and disobedience to the Lord.

The Lord is so particular how we observe His Sabbath that He takes into account even our conversation on His holy day. In Isaiah 58:13 He instructs that on His holy day we are not to speak our own words, meaning that on the Sabbath we should avoid ordinary conversation concerning secular matters, which is entirely proper on the six working days.

No one can obey God's Sabbath commands except a born-again Christian, who has Christ dwelling within and controlling his mind and affections. Only a truly converted person can keep the Sabbath holy, for there is a decided difference between being a Saturday-keeper and a real Sabbathkeeper. A nominal Christian, or even an unbeliever, may be a Saturday-keeper by laying aside his ordinary work on Saturday and attending church regularly. But no one can keep the Sabbath holy unless Christ's sanctifying presence lives within him.

Accepting the Biblical evidences that the seventh day is the only right day to keep can make a person a Saturday-keeper, but nothing except the converting power of Christ in addition to the acceptance of Bible evidence can make a person a Christian Sabbathkeeper. Genuine obedience comes only from a renewed heart when the mind is merged into the mind of Christ. Then keeping the Sabbath and obeying God's law will not be burdensome. On the contrary, it will be a true, abiding joy. But trying to keep Saturday without the love of Christ in the heart is drudgery.

Jesus gave us an example to follow. (1 Peter 2:21.) It was part of His life to attend worship at God's house every Sabbath (Luke 4:16), and so it will form a part of our way of life when we follow Jesus' example.

Jesus said, "It is lawful to do well on the sabbath days." Matthew 12:12. Therefore, relieving the afflicted and performing deeds of kindness and necessity accord with this principle. A safe rule is, Do not leave any work to do on the Sabbath that you can accomplish during the six working days.

Isaiah 58:13 joins true Sabbathkeeping and delighting oneself in the Lord. The Sabbath should be the most joyful, the sweetest, and the most blessed day of the week.

Every Sabbath holds a triple significance. First, it points back to the institution of the Sabbath in perfect Eden, where no sorrow, trouble, sickness, or death marred human existence. Perfect joy reigned supreme. It reminds us that if man had not sinned, the world would still be free from all trouble and sorrow.

Thus the Sabbath of Christ embraces some of the love and joy of the original, perfect creation. It has in it a breath of Eden, and true Sabbath observance recaptures some of the delight of the first Sabbath in a perfect world.

Second, the Sabbath delightfully points forward to the glorious restoration in the coming new earth where all will honor the Sabbath forever. Every Sabbath foreshadows the Paradise restored where sin, sickness, sorrow, and death will be no more. As each week rolls by, the successive Sabbaths are like lights along the way leading to the eternal city.

> "Day of all the week the best,
> Emblem of eternal rest.
>
> .   .   .   .
>
> Here afford us, Lord, a taste
> Of our everlasting feast."

The third delightful aspect is that as the Sabbath comes in, our minds are drawn with a special emphasis to Christ, the Creator, who made the world in six days and rested upon the seventh. We joyfully look upward to the Omnipotent Creator and Saviour, who saves to the uttermost. It enables us to enter more fully the joy and love of creation and redemption in Christ. It bears witness to our souls that the same Christ who made the world in six days has, by His creative power, re-created us spiritually into new persons and is sanctifying us in preparation for His second advent.

Remembering the Sabbath to keep it holy is not limited to the twenty-four-hour period on the last day of the week. We must remember the Sabbath in our plans, appointments, and transactions during the other six days so that we shall leave nothing out of line with God's holy day when it arrives each week.

Sabbath observance projects itself into the entire week and into our everyday relationship to our Creator-Redeemer. Thus it helps keep the Lord always before us. This first word of the Sabbath precept—"remember"—must exert a molding influence on our lives every day.

Especially must we remember the Sabbath on Friday, the "preparation" day. (Mark 15:42; Exodus 16:22-28.) God intends that we use Friday to prepare for the Sabbath, for unless we care for certain temporal and business items on Friday, we cannot keep the Sabbath holy.

We should plan all Friday's work with reference to the Sabbath, and any business or secular work that we cannot complete before Friday sunset should remain undone until after the Sabbath. Using Friday, the preparation day, correctly enables us to welcome the Sabbath immediately when it arrives. Also it prevents certain worldly affairs from causing us to miss the mark which God has set for Sabbath-keeping.

Everyone should carefully examine himself and evaluate His relationship to Christ and His Sabbath. Do I keep the Sabbath in a manner that truly binds me closer to the Creator-Redeemer? Does it bring me the joys and delights of His loving presence in an extra measure, above that which I enjoy during the other six days? Is it like a bit of heaven let down to earth, or is it like being confined and restricted in a cell? Is it a delight, or is it drudgery?

"If thou turn away thy foot from the sabbath, from doing thy pleasure on my holy day; and call the sabbath a delight, the holy of the Lord, honourable; and shalt honour him, not doing thine own ways, nor finding thine own pleasure, nor speaking thine own words: then shalt thou delight thyself in the Lord; and I will cause thee to ride upon the high places of the earth, and feed thee with the heritage of Jacob thy father: for the mouth of the Lord hath spoken it." Isaiah 58:13, 14.

God makes three promises here to those who truly hallow His Sabbath: "Then shalt thou delight thyself in the Lord"—true and abiding happiness; "I will cause thee to ride upon the high places of the earth"—spiritual prosperity; and "[I will] feed thee with the heritage of Jacob thy father" —an eternal home in the new earth.

The word *heritage* means "an estate that passes by descent or an inheritance"; and the inheritance of Jacob is the inheritance of Isaac his father, which is the inheritance of his father Abraham. The real inheritance of Abraham is the new earth (Romans 4:13; Hebrews 11:13-16), and those who truly belong to Christ are heirs to this inheritance also. (Galatians 3:29.)

What greater promise could God make to those who hallow His Sabbath than the inheritance of Jacob, Isaac, and Abraham—an eternal home in the new earth, one free from all sickness, sorrow, trouble, and death?

Note the parallelism in Isaiah 58:13, 14. The fulfillment of God's three promises is conditioned on three aspects of Sabbath observance: "not doing thine own ways," "nor finding thine own pleasure," "nor speaking thine own words."

The first of these, "not doing thine own ways," means refraining from doing work on the Sabbath such as we do on the other six days. Instead of following our own ways, we follow God's appointed way for proper Sabbathkeeping.

The second, "not finding thine own pleasure," means that the Sabbath is not for picnics, merrymaking, sightseeing, or ordinary travel. Instead of seeking our own pleasure, we should follow God's good pleasure on His day.

The third, "nor speaking thine own words," indicates that on the Sabbath we should refrain from talking about worldly things or engaging in light conversation. Talking upon anything or everything which may come into the mind is speaking our own words. We must discipline our minds to dwell upon sacred themes.

Carelessness in Sabbathkeeping begets carelessness in other areas of God's requirements for our talking, eating, drinking, dressing, associations, recreations, etc. God's requirements for proper Sabbath observance are all for our own good so that we may receive additional strength from Christ to live better during the week just ahead.

10

THE SIGN OF RIGHTEOUSNESS BY FAITH

"Righteousness by faith" is God's solution to your greatest problem—the sin problem. How can all your past sins be remitted? And how can you be kept from sin thereafter? Or, to put it another way, how can you get right with God and then stay right?

Only a twofold application of the perfect righteousness of Christ will solve this twofold sin problem. The moment you receive the Lord Jesus as your personal Saviour and in penitence surrender your heart in obedience to Him, His imputed righteousness cancels all your past sins. Then as you continually surrender to Christ, He lives in you every day, imparting His righteousness to keep you from sin.

His imputed righteousness for justification (His righteousness put to your heavenly account) and His imparted righteousness for sanctification (His righteousness daily shared with you) constitute righteousness by faith in capsule form.

What has keeping the seventh day to do with righteousness by faith? The Lord gives the answer in Exodus 31:13: "Verily my sabbaths ye shall keep: for it is a sign between me and you . . . that ye may know that I am the Lord that doth sanctify you."

The Lord emphasizes in these words that He alone can save and sanctify the believer, which forms the heart of righteousness by faith. God says that keeping His Sabbath properly signifies sanctification. It serves as a continuing sign that the Lord is sanctifying the believer every day.

Make no mistake about it. Observing the right day of itself does not or cannot confer an acceptable righteousness on the Sabbathkeeper. Only Christ can do this in response to our faith in Him as our personal Saviour. He was made to be sin for us, so that we might be made the righteousness of God in Him. (2 Corinthians 5:21.)

However, the Scriptures do say that keeping the right day—the seventh day as set apart by Christ—is a sign of Christ's righteousness that He imputes and imparts to the believer. Furthermore, the righteousness of Christ manifests itself in obedience to all God's commandments. (Romans 8:3, 4; 10:4.) It cannot do otherwise, because He personally obeyed the commandments.

Hallowing the Sabbath is the natural fruitage of the righteousness of Christ in justification and sanctification and signifies that God has delivered us from the bondage of sin. Thus Moses, in referring to the Sabbath commandment, mentioned that God had delivered Israel from bondage in Egypt and said, "Therefore the Lord thy God commanded thee to keep the sabbath day." (Deuteronomy 5:12-15.)

A previous chapter emphasized that the Sabbath does not signify sanctification in one who keeps the seventh day unless Christ is justifying and sanctifying him through faith, for in true Sabbathkeeping the believer does not keep the Sabbath to make himself righteous, but he keeps it because he has received and is receiving the perfect righteousness of Christ.

An apple tree does not become an apple tree by bearing apples. It first has to be an apple tree. Then the apples come as a natural fruitage. So the true Christian does not keep the Sabbath or obey the other nine precepts to make himself righteous. Rather, this is the natural fruitage of the righteousness Christ shares with him. He who keeps the Sabbath in this way is not a legalist, for the outward keeping of the seventh day betokens the believer's inner experience in justification and sanctification. Hence, the true Sabbathkeeper does not refrain from forbidden actions on the Sabbath in order to win God's favor but because he loves God and wants to make the Sabbath count for the most for closer fellowship with God.

The Sabbath as a sign of Christ as the Creator and the Redeemer brings home to the soul that he is completely dependent upon Christ for every breath and heartbeat. No man can keep alive his own soul. In the Creator we have our life and being.

Sabbathkeeping impresses upon us that only He who created us can save us. His righteousness alone can make us what we ought to be. It lays the glory of man in the dust of selfless living. At the foot of the cross we kneel in full surrender. "Nothing in my hand I bring, Simply to Thy cross I cling."

True Sabbathkeeping continually safeguards against pride, self-sufficiency, self-righteousness, materialism, formalism, and ingratitude. It reciprocates a loving response from the converted heart to the love of God in creation and redemption.

Unfortunately, countless thousands of sincere Christians have turned against keeping the seventh day by fallacious reasoning which asserts it goes contrary to salvation by grace alone. They are told that the New Testament in Galatians and other places condemns any type of legalistic day keeping and that Sabbath observance is legalism, which Christians should shun lest they fall from grace.

Let us inquire, What is legalism? Legalism attempts to earn salvation by individual effort. It is conforming to the law and certain observances as a means of justification before God. This is wrong, because "by the deeds of the law there shall no flesh be justified in his sight." (Romans 3:20.)

Justification comes only through faith in Christ (Romans 3:28); but in direct connection with this, the Word of God declares that justification by faith alone does not make void the keeping of the moral law. On the contrary, it establishes obedience to the Ten Commandments as the natural expression of the righteousness of Christ in the life of the justified person. (See Romans 3:31; 8:3, 4.)

Those who denounce Sabbath observance as legalism need to consider this: If a born-again Christian refrains from worshiping false gods and maintains reverence as commanded by the first and third precepts, is he opposed to salvation by grace? Are purity, honesty, and truthfulness, as advocated by the seventh, eighth, and ninth commandments, opposed to free grace? The answer is No to both questions. Even so the keeping of the seventh day by a renewed soul is not legalism, nor is it contrary to salvation only by grace. In fact, the Sabbath commandment is the only precept in the law that stands as a sign of deliverance from sin and sanctification by grace alone.

True Sabbathkeeping is hallowing the seventh day as an everlasting memorial of Christ the Creator and only Saviour. Therefore it signifies that the individual cannot save himself even as he could not have created himself. Honoring the seventh day as a sign of sanctification is a token of the impartation of Christ's righteousness—the very opposite of legalism and Judaizing.

Surely, it is manifestly unsound for those who oppose the seventh day to admit that a Christian should live in harmony with the other nine of the Ten Commandments. "For whosoever shall keep the whole law, and yet offend in one point, he is guilty of all." James 2:10. The Christian who lives by faith in Christ's righteousness will obey all the commandments. (1 John 2:3, 4; Psalm 40:8.)

All that the New Testament says against legalism and Judaizing may be reduced to four propositions:

1. The Jewish ceremonial laws regarding circumcision, meat and drink offerings, the observance of yearly sabbath days connected with the Feast of Unleavened Bread, Pentecost, the Feast of Tabernacles, the Day of Atonement, etc., were not binding after the cross. None of them were to be imposed upon the Gentile converts to Christianity.

2. Justification and salvation are only by faith in Christ.

3. The Ten Commandments must not be kept as a means of salvation.

4. Under the new covenant, Christ writes the Decalogue upon the heart of the pardoned and converted person so that he is under the jurisdiction of this law in Christ.

But take note that nothing in all this condemns keeping the seventh day, for it is a sign of Jesus as the Creator and only Redeemer.

The Sabbath harmonizes with salvation by grace alone, for keeping it as Jesus kept it signifies righteousness by faith.

The Jews perverted the Sabbath until it became a sign of righteousness by works—just the opposite of what God designed it to be. Keeping the seventh day with the wrong motivation and without a proper experience in the Lord stands as part of the wrong system of salvation by works, but keeping the seventh day as a sign of true sanctification is part of salvation by grace alone.

This is not a case of blowing hot and cold on the same issue. Prayer, church attendance, deeds of charity, tithing, and giving liberal offerings may form a part of legalism and righteousness by works if they are done to earn salvation. Conversely, if prompted by love and the fruitage of Christ dwelling within, these same good deeds become a part of salvation by grace.

Paul emphasized that a faith working by love is what really counts. "For in Jesus Christ neither circumcision availeth any thing, nor uncircumcision; but faith which worketh by love." Galatians 5:6. When we have such a faith, we don't keep the commandments merely because we "have to" but because our love makes obedience a delight.

Ask yourself: "Do I keep the Sabbath merely because I have to or because I love to do it?" Your answer may reveal whether you are following righteousness by faith or righteousness by works.

While it is good to obey God from a realization of obligation, it is better to have the love of God in the heart to the extent that we obey because we truly want to do it. True Sabbathkeeping is a token of mutual love between our best Friend and us. (John 14:21.)

He who loves God wants above all else to obey Christ. He does not need to be pushed into obedience. The love of Christ motivates him to obey. His controlling desire is, "I delight to do thy will, O my God: yea, thy law is within my heart." Psalm 40:8.

A probing query comes home to the soul: "Do I obey Jesus and keep His Sabbath from a controlling desire born of divine love? Or is it chiefly from the compulsion of divine law?"

Some argue that keeping Sunday in honor of Christ's resurrection is part of righteousness by faith and that any keeping of the seventh day is righteousness by works. Yet we have shown that nowhere does the Bible authorize keeping the first day of the week in honor of our Lord's resurrection. The Bible teaches that the substitution of man-made institutions and rules in place of God's is one of the many forms of autosalvation, or the false system of righteousness by works. "In vain they do worship me, teaching for doctrines the commandments of men." Matthew 15:9. So, in actuality, the substitution of the man-made Sunday day of worship in place of the Christ-appointed seventh-day Sabbath forms one of the false principles of righteousness by works.

The heart of righteousness by faith is the application to the trusting and surrendered believer of Christ's justifying and sanctifying righteousness, and true Sabbathkeeping signifies that we have received and are receiving this righteousness. It keeps before us in proper perspective our creature-Creator and redeemed-Redeemer relationship. Thus the Sabbath helps us become Christ-centered instead of self-centered.

The Jews mistakenly observed the letter of the law while missing the spirit of the law. Their religion in the time of Christ and His apostles had degenerated into an outward observance of the letter of the law to merit salvation, with little vision of the deeper, inner spirit of the law. In direct contrast, true Christianity goes far beyond the letter of the law and produces obedience to the spirit of the law. Such obedience is not a means of salvation but is the fruit of the operation of grace in the life. Paul alluded to this when he declared that Christians should live in the newness of the spirit and not in the oldness of the letter. (Romans 7:6.)

Some Christians claim that living in the newness of the

spirit rather than in the oldness of the letter means that one may violate the letter of the Decalogue and still obey it in spirit. They apply this false reasoning to the Sabbath commandment and claim that "not in the oldness of the letter" implies that Christians need not observe the exact day as specified in the command. They feel that Sunday observance carries out the spirit of the law.

Chapter 7—"Does It Make Any Difference?"—showed that such an idea contradicts God's Word. Suffice it to add here that a person may follow the letter of the law and not obey its spirit, but no one who obeys the law in spirit will live contrary to the letter. The command "Thou shalt not kill" exemplifies this fact. If he loves his enemies and his neighbor as himself—the spirit of the sixth commandment —he will never violate the letter.

Consider the eighth commandment, "Thou shalt not steal." The spirit of this command is, "Be honest." He who is honest will not steal. He who obeys the law in spirit will not live contrary to the letter. The spirit of the law means keeping it in its fullest and deepest sense.

Hence, this matter of living according to the newness of the spirit and not in the oldness of the letter does not make keeping the seventh day any less binding. It does involve true Sabbathkeeping, however, as practiced by Jesus, who fulfilled both the spirit and the letter.

The spirit of true Sabbathkeeping reveals a supreme love for Jesus Christ, the Creator and Saviour, who is making us into new persons. It makes the keeping of the right day in the right way a sign of righteousness by faith.

Ellen G. White has written, "To those who keep holy the Sabbath day it is the sign of sanctification. True sanctification is harmony with God, oneness with Him in character. It is received through obedience to those principles that are the transcript of His character. And the Sabbath is the sign of obedience. *He who from the heart obeys the fourth commandment will obey the whole law."*—*Testimonies,* Vol. 6, p. 350. (Italics supplied.)

The Sabbath, as the sign of the Creator, is the seal of the Decalogue. A seal imparts validity to a document and for many years was comparable to a signature. The seals or signatures of the grantors at the bottom of a grant deed validate what is recited in the deed. So true Sabbathkeeping serves as a seal of one's obedience to all the other commandments by projecting itself into every day of the week and into the other commandments.

"We are to understand its spiritual bearing upon all the transactions of life. All who regard the Sabbath as a sign between them and God, showing that He is the God who sanctifies them, will represent the principles of His government. They will bring into daily practice the law of His kingdom. Daily it will be their prayer that the sanctification of the Sabbath may rest upon them. Every day they will have the companionship of Christ and will exemplify the perfection of His character."—*Ibid.,* pp. 353, 354.

Countless thousands of sincere Christians have accepted Christ and His righteousness while honestly keeping Sunday, because they think it is a part of the way of Jesus. But when they are convinced from the Scriptures that Christ has appointed His seventh-day Sabbath as a sign that He is Creator and Sanctifier, their love for Christ will lead them to gladly accept His Sabbath. They will recognize that Sabbath observance is a natural, logical, essential part of accepting Christ as their Lord and Saviour, for the full gospel includes keeping Christ's Sabbath.

11

WHY NOT FOUND OUT BEFORE?

In view of how plainly the Bible sets forth the seventh day as the only right day to keep, why have nearly all Christians lost sight of the Scriptural doctrine? Why didn't men of God like Luther, Calvin, Knox, and Wesley accept the Sabbath?

If I would ask you, "Why don't people in Michigan pick ripe peaches off their trees in January?" what would you answer? You would most likely reply, "January is not the time for it. The trees may be half buried in snow. The trees will fruit at the right time."

So it is with the Sabbath truth. Certain Biblical predictions indicated that a widespread departure from the truth would prevail for many centuries after the apostles passed away. Then in the closing age God would restore the forgotten truths.

Paul, Peter, John, and the other apostles, along with the Christians in their day, dedicatedly followed the example and teachings of the Lord Jesus Christ (1 Corinthians 11:1; 1 Peter 2:21) by keeping the seventh day holy.

Paul predicted that false teachers would arise after his death and would mingle error with Christian truths. (Acts 20:29, 30; 2 Thessalonians 2:3-5.) After the apostles had passed away, many in the church began to lose sight of some of the teachings of Jesus and the apostles. Rites, ceremonies, and customs which Jesus and His apostles never taught crept into use. Later, these practices were urged upon the believers as being of divine authority. One of these was the honoring of Sunday in commemoration of the resurrection of Christ.

Scholars generally recognize that during the first and second centuries, Christians did not keep Sunday as a day of rest. They did meet for worship but then went about their vocations. As time passed, Sunday began to take on more and more of the aspects of a day of rest until it generally replaced the seventh-day Sabbath of the Ten Commandments.

Some have asked, If the seventh day is the right day, why do nearly all Christians keep the first day? It is because in the early years of the Christian church certain Christians, without any Bible authority, transferred the day of rest from Saturday to Sunday. Centuries of usage have established it among nearly all Christians.

Why do the present generation of Protestants keep Sunday? The present generation keep Sunday because their fathers before them worshiped on Sunday. Why did their fathers before them keep Sunday? Because their fathers before them observed Sunday. And so on until you come to that time when certain Christians coming out of the Roman Catholic Church to form the first Protestant churches brought Sunday-keeping with them. They discarded the false doctrines of purgatory, penance, the worship of Mary, confessing to a priest, etc., but they did not discard Sunday observance, which rests solely on the authority of the Catholic Church even as these other doctrines.

Such an extensive departure from the truth in post-apostolic times and the ascendance of these errors for centuries necessitate a restoration, and such a reformatory movement for the recovery of these lost truths is clearly predicted in Bible prophecy.

Six Biblical prophecies concurrently predict the restoration of the Sabbath and other lost truths in the closing period of history. Two of these are found in Isaiah and stress keeping the right day in the right way. The first—Isaiah 56:1, 2 —calls on men to stop polluting the Sabbath. The second— Isaiah 58:12-14—refers to the Sabbath being trodden underfoot. Although these statements primarily refer to a Sabbath reformation in the time of Isaiah, they also seem to apply to a similar restoration in our day.

Note this description: "And they that shall be of thee shall build the old waste places: thou shalt raise up the foundations of many generations; and thou shalt be called, The repairer of the breach, The restorer of paths to dwell in. If thou turn away thy foot from the sabbath, from doing thy pleasure on my holy day . . ." Isaiah 58:12, 13.

Rebuilding the old waste places and raising up the foundations of former generations forecast a recovery of neglected and buried truths. They imply a return to the original truths given to God's church in the Bible.

At Williamsburg, Virginia, men have raised up the foundations of the colonial way of life in America. So in these last days God's message will raise up His eternal way as He revealed it to His people in the teachings of Jesus and His apostles.

"The restorer of paths to dwell in" means walking in the

old paths (compare Jeremiah 6:16)—the law of truth and righteousness as proclaimed from heaven at Sinai. The Rotherham translation renders this phrase in Isaiah 58:12, "A Restorer of paths leading home." The path of obedience to Christ's commandments does lead home. "Blessed are they that do his commandments, that they may have right to the tree of life, and may enter in through the gates into the city." Revelation 22:14.

"The repairer of the breach" refers to a restoration of the true Sabbath to its rightful place in the practice of Christians. Repairing the breach implies taking one's foot off the Sabbath and keeping it as the Lord directs in verse 13.

Most people trample the Sabbath by using it as an ordinary day instead of honoring it as the Lord's holy rest day, and God calls to them, "Take your foot off My Sabbath and keep it holy."

The substitution of Sunday-keeping in place of the seventh day makes a breach in one's full commitment to the Creator-Saviour and His law. But those who keep the seventh day as the Lord has directed repair this breach.

Different religious bodies teach conflicting theories concerning God's law, but they all agree that Christians should live according to all the Ten Commandments except the one which specifies observance of the seventh day. Doesn't this plainly show that the breach is the setting aside of Sabbathkeeping?

Today much is said concerning the need of bridging, or removing, "the generation gap," "the credibility gap," "the educational gap," "the opportunity gap," and "the poverty gap," and they need remedying. But the gap most needing a remedy is the commandment gap—the rejected Sabbath command.

God is looking for men and women who will "stand in the gap" (Ezekiel 22:30), and His people obey His call.

Hence, His true church for our day is distinguished by those who repair this breach in His Sabbath commandment.

The third of the six concurrent prophecies of Sabbath restoration is Revelation 7:1-3, which forecasts a special Sabbath-restoring message in the closing period of history. God will place His seal, or Sabbath sign, of obedience to His commandments upon the foreheads, or minds, of His servants.

The fourth forecast of a special vindication of God's downtrodden Sabbath is found in Daniel 8:12-14. Daniel foretold a departure from the truth that would prevail under the long reign of the papal power over Christendom.

Verse 12 says, "It cast down the truth to the ground." What is meant by "the truth"? The teachings of Jesus are the truth (John 8:45, 46, 31, 32; 14:6), as is also the gospel of Christ as preached by the apostles (Galatians 3:1; 2:14; 1 Peter 1:22). The Sabbath of Christ as a sign that He is the Creator-Redeemer is an indispensable feature of the truth. So the Sabbath in particular is a leading item of the truth which this Roman power cast to the ground.

Daniel 7:25 predicts that this same power would attempt to "change times and laws." In fulfillment of this prophecy, apostate Christendom attempted to change the fourth commandment by setting aside the seventh day as Christ commanded and setting up Sunday in its place.

Daniel 8:13, 14 tells of a restoration of these downtrodden truths. The question is posed, "How long will the truth be cast down to the ground? How long will it be buried under false teachings and hidden from view? When will these lost truths be restored to their rightful place?"

God's answer is recorded in verse 14: "And he said unto me, Unto two thousand and three hundred days; then shall the sanctuary be cleansed." God indicates that He would inaugurate a restoration at the end of 2300 days, which represent 2300 years on the basis of the confirmed year-day principle in Biblical prophecy. (Ezekiel 4:6; Numbers 14:34.)

Daniel 9:24 shows that this 2300-day-year period comprises two parts: seventy weeks, or 490 day-years allotted to the Jews, as the chosen nation, and a remaining period of 1810 day-years, at the end of which the restoration of an important truth would come in connection with the cleansing of the sanctuary.

Daniel 9:25 establishes the beginning point from which to compute these periods. When this prophecy was given, the Jews were captives in Babylon and Jerusalem was in ruins. So this prophecy foretold that in due time a decree would be issued to restore the Jewish state at Jerusalem. Ezra 7:11-28 records this decree. Artaxerxes, king of Persia, issued it in his seventh year—457 B.C. (Ezra 7:6-9.)

Four hundred and ninety years from 457 B.C. extend to A.D. 34, the end of the seventy prophetic weeks. From A.D. 34 the remaining 1810 day-years extend to 1844 as the terminal date of the 2300 prophetic days.

The restoration of the headquarters of the religion of the only true God signaled the beginning of the 2300 days. The end of this period in 1844 was to be marked by the inauguration of a movement for the restoration of the truth that apostate Christianity had cast down to the ground.

The question comes, What happened in 1844 in relationship to this prophecy of Daniel 8:14? Did a movement arise for the restoration of these neglected and buried truths? These questions the next chapter will answer.

Bible students generally recognize that the books of Daniel and Revelation are counterparts. Daniel 8:12-14 fits into Revelation 14:6-12, which presents a fuller picture of a renaissance Sabbath movement between 1844 and the end of this present gospel age. Revelation 14:6-12 is the fifth of these six concurrent Scriptural forecasts of a restoration of the true Sabbath in our day.

This symbolical prophecy portrays three angels whose preaching of a threefold message to every nation leads directly to the second coming of Christ as pictured in Revelation 14:14-16. Clearly these three angels' messages are God's last message to humanity.

Four parts of this threefold message predict a worldwide proclamation of the Sabbath truth:

1. Those who accept the threefold message are distinguished from other peoples by their adherence to the commandments of God and the faith of Jesus. Thus we read in Revelation 14:12, "Here is the patience of the saints: here are *they that keep the commandments of God, and the faith of Jesus.*" Since they keep the commandments, they will observe the seventh-day Sabbath as required by the fourth commandment.

2. This final gospel message calls upon all to "worship him that made heaven, and earth." (Revelation 14:7.) What has God appointed for us to do to indicate that we worship Him as Creator? Scripture reveals that keeping the seventh-day Sabbath is the sign of Christ, the Creator of heaven and earth.

3. This threefold message also warns mankind not to worship the beast and his image (Revelation 14:9), revealing that the main testing issue under this final phase of the gospel is the worship of Christ as the Creator versus the worship of the beast and his image. It seems apparent that the worship of the beast and his image involves directly the opposite of the worship of Christ as the Creator.

Since the Bible shows that the right observance of the seventh day is the distinguishing mark of worshiping the Creator, the worship of the beast and his image must involve keeping the first day, or Sunday, as a man-made substitute.

4. Also this message warns all against receiving the mark of the beast. (Revelation 14:9, 10.) Those who heed this warning and adhere to the commandments of God and the faith of Jesus will receive the seal of God upon their foreheads. (Revelation 7:1-3.) The main testing issue is the reception of the seal of God versus the mark of the beast.

We have shown from Exodus 31:13 and Ezekiel 20:12, 20 that the right observance of the Sabbath is a sign or seal of Christian sanctification. True Sabbathkeeping is a divine seal of righteousness by faith and full conformity to God's will. The mark of the beast, as the opposite of the seal of God, must involve obedience to apostate Christendom in keeping Sunday as the substitute for the Sabbath. God is calling out a people in every country who will keep His commandments, including the Sabbath commandment, which means a restoration of the neglected Sabbath.

This Sabbath-restoring message is introduced with the stirring call, "Fear God, and give glory to him; for the hour of his judgment is come." God appointed that the threefold message would begin its work when the hour of God's judgment arrived in heaven.

Daniel 8:14 and related scriptures pinpoint the year 1844 as the time when the investigative phase of the judgment began in heaven. The cleansing of the sanctuary (Daniel 8:14) began at the end of the 2300 day-years, or in 1844. The Bible teaches that the beginning of the cleansing of the heavenly sanctuary synchronizes with the beginning of the hour of God's judgment.

The people of God looked upon the Day of Atonement when the earthly sanctuary was cleansed as a day of judgment. Since the typical is always fulfilled in the antitypical, the cleansing of the heavenly sanctuary, inaugurated in 1844, implies that the investigative phase of God's judgment of the professed righteous began in 1844.

Revelation 14:7 shows that the arrival of the hour of God's judgment marks the rise of the Sabbath reformatory movement of this threefold message. The Word of God is always fulfilled in its season. In 1844 at the appointed time this Sabbathkeeping reform movement began its work. It is repairing the breach by proclaiming to all the world that the Sabbath is the sign of the Creator-Redeemer.

The sixth of these concurrent prophecies of a restoration of the true Sabbath to its rightful place in the gospel of Christ is found in Revelation 12:17, which forecasts that in the closing period of history God will have a people who keep the commandments of God and have the testimony of Jesus Christ. Obviously, since they obey God's commandments, they will be seventh-day-Sabbath-keeping Christians.

The commandment-keeping "remnant" of Revelation 12:17 are identical with the commandment-keeping people of Revelation 14:12. Thus the time of the remnant is the same as the time for the threefold message, which is, as we have shown, from 1844 to Christ's second advent.

Six prophecies—Isaiah 56:1-8; 58:12-14; Revelation 7:1-3; Daniel 8:12-14; Revelation 14:6-12; 12:17—predict a worldwide Sabbath reformation before Christ returns. Seventh-day Adventists believe they are fulfilling these prophecies.

12

HOW TO FIND THE TRUE RELIGION

Many different denominations teach many different doctrines, and proponents of each urge that their particular way is the only right way. The wise man observed, "Every way of a man is right in his own eyes." Proverbs 21:2.

We must never forget that the God of all truth has declared that we must not follow merely what is right in our own eyes but that we are to adhere to "that which is good and right in the sight of the Lord thy God." (Deuteronomy 12:8, 28.) The only way to be sure of the Lord's way for religion is to discover it in the Bible.

The numerous discordant theories in religion confuse and perplex many people, and Mr. Average Man wonders, "In view of all these conflicting interpretations and doctrines, how can I ever be sure which is the Lord's way for me?"

The Bible shows that the surest evidence that a respective teaching is the true way of the Lord is if it presents the message God has appointed in His Word to be preached, believed, and obeyed at that time.

Here are some Biblical illustrations of this ultimate test of the truth:

It is the Sabbath day in old Nazareth. The synagogue is filled with worshipers, and Jesus is about to preach His first sermon to His fellow townsmen. Each wonders, Who is this carpenter who claims to be the Son of God? Is He really the promised Messiah who can save us? Or is He a would-be prophet with theories of His own devising?

The ruler of the synagogue hands Him the roll containing the prophecy of Isaiah. He opens the scroll and begins to read a passage which stands as the strongest evidence of His Messiahship.

"And when he had opened the book, he found the place where it was written, The Spirit of the Lord is upon me, because he hath anointed me to preach the gospel to the poor; he hath sent me to heal the brokenhearted, to preach deliverance to the captives, and recovering of sight to the blind, to set at liberty them that are bruised, to preach the acceptable year of the Lord. And he closed the book, and he gave it again to the minister, and sat down. And the eyes of all them that were in the synagogue were fastened on him." Luke 4:17-20.

God had given this prophecy to Israel seven hundred years before. Isaiah had foretold what the Messiah would do when He appeared and the very message He would preach—a message that would heal the brokenhearted and set men free from the bondage of sin.

The hour had struck for its fulfillment. The Carpenter of Nazareth was doing and preaching precisely what Isaiah's Messianic prophecy had declared. So Jesus told them, "This day is this scripture fulfilled in your ears." The fulfillment of these Messianic prophecies in Jesus of Nazareth constitutes the strongest and surest evidence that He is indeed the Promised Deliverer, the Christ, the Son of the Living God. On another occasion Jesus used these various Messianic predictions to reconfirm the faith of His disciples in His Messiahship when they had almost lost their faith after His crucifixion. (Luke 24:13-27, 44, 45.)

Jesus showed that when a Scriptural prophecy was fulfilled in a certain teaching, it was what God had appointed for that respective time and formed the strongest possible evidence of the authenticity of those teachings. We cannot improve Christ's methods of presenting the truth. The best way to find the true religion is to discover from the Bible the message that God has appointed for man to follow.

Here is another illustration from the Bible. Turn back the pages of history to that momentous hour when God's Messiah was about to be manifested to His people. Great crowds are flocking into the wilderness to hear a new preacher with a startling message.

Questions naturally arise concerning the authenticity of his teachings, and many wonder, How can we be sure that his teachings are the right way for us to follow in preference to that of the established religious parties? Finally, a deputation from the accepted religious authorities interrogates him concerning the authority for his teachings.

"And this is the record of John, when the Jews sent priests and Levites from Jerusalem to ask him, Who art thou?

"And he confessed, and denied not; but confessed, I am not the Christ.

"And they asked him, What then? Art thou Elias? And he saith, I am not. Art thou that prophet? And he answered, No.

"Then said they unto him, Who art thou? that we may give an answer to them that sent us. What sayest thou of thyself?" John 1:19-22.

What evidence did John cite to establish that his teachings were the right way for the people to follow? He cited the precise prophecy in Isaiah which his message fulfilled.

"He said, I am the voice of one crying in the wilderness, Make straight the way of the Lord, as said the prophet Esaias." John 1:23.

Seven hundred years before, God had foretold in Isaiah 40:3 that before the Messiah appeared to Israel, He would send a special message to prepare His way. There would be the voice of one crying in the wilderness, "Prepare ye the way of the Lord."

Now the hour had struck for this seven-hundred-year-old prophecy to be fulfilled. God had raised up John the Baptist at the right time to preach this message showing the right way to take. There could be no mistake. John the Baptist preached the message God had appointed for that time.

There were at that time various religious sects among the Jews. The Bible mentions some of them: the Pharisees, Sadducees, and Herodians. But the fulfillment of Isaiah 40:3 in John's work and mission was a positive evidence that his teachings were what the Lord wanted people to do in preference to the other religious ways. The evidence was conclusive because none of these other sects preached what God called for in Isaiah 40:3.

Now the question comes, Among all these divergent religious teachings in our day, is there one that can present the same type of conclusive evidence which John cited in behalf of his teachings? Most assuredly there is. Revelation 14:6-12 sets forth God's message for this closing period of history. The context indicates that this threefold message prepares the way for the second advent of our Lord even as

God called John the Baptist to prepare the way for Christ's first advent.

God portrays three angels preaching to every nation. Each proclaims part of a united threefold message. Now, the Bible definitely states that the preaching of God's truth to every nation is to be accomplished through men and women (Mark 16:15) rather than by the audible voices of angels. Therefore these three angels with their threefold gospel message for every nation represent a body of men and women who will proclaim these truths to all the world.

Furthermore, Revelation 14:12 identifies them: "Here are they that keep the commandments of God, and the faith of Jesus." Since they keep the commandments of God, they are a seventh-day-Sabbath Christian people.

As we read on in Revelation 14, we find that the *next event after this threefold message goes to every nation is the second advent of Christ, as described in verse 14:* "And I looked, and behold a white cloud, and upon the cloud one sat like unto the Son of man, having on his head a golden crown, and in his hand a sharp sickle."

The preaching of this threefold message leads directly into the appearing of Christ to reap the harvest of the gospel —positive evidence that it represents the Lord's will for every soul just before His return.

It constitutes God's present truth for this present time, the final phase of His everlasting gospel, fully appropriate and supremely essential for this time-of-the-end period. What a sobering incentive to make sure that we fully accept it!

In the previous chapter we learned that this Sabbath reform movement began in 1844 when the hour of God's judgment arrived. This closing age between 1844 and the second coming of Christ is God's appointed time for the Sabbath-restoring message of Revelation 14:6-12.

Did such a movement begin in 1844? Has it become a worldwide movement as called for in Revelation 14:6? Does it teach the truths set forth in this God-appointed message for our day? Bible prophecy never fails to be fulfilled in its season. "The scripture cannot be broken."

In 1844 at Washington, New Hampshire, a company of about forty Christians who expected the return of Christ discovered from the Bible that they were keeping the wrong day. They could find no Biblical authority for Sunday-keeping. So they began to keep Saturday. Soon, in adjoining states, other Christians who also awaited Christ's coming, accepted the Sabbath, and in 1860 these Sabbathkeeping Adventists chose the name "Seventh-day Adventist."

From this small beginning in 1844, Seventh-day Adventism has proclaimed the true Sabbath around the world. Now over two million strong, this movement for restoring the true Sabbath has not arisen by the design or plans of men but because of God's predetermined plan as expressed in these Biblical prophecies.

God has fulfilled Revelation 14:6-12 by raising up the Seventh-day Adventist Church, which is proclaiming the way of Jesus for this time in direct fulfillment of those six concurrent prophecies for the restoration of the true Sabbath.

John the Baptist would not have arisen when he did and preached what he proclaimed had it not been for the forecast in Isaiah 40:3. Even so, this Sabbath reform movement of Seventh-day Adventism would not have begun in 1844 had it not been for the forecast in Revelation 14:6-12. The Sabbath reform movement of the Adventist people came at the right time with the right message to show the right way for God's people to follow at this time.

Their teachings and work represent the three angels' messages, which prepare the way for our Lord's second advent as John's preaching prepared the way for His first advent. The Adventist people proclaim the very message God has appointed for this time, and this constitutes the strongest possible evidence that the Adventist way of religion is the Lord's appointment in clear distinction from every one of the numerous religious ways clamoring for our support. *Thus, the Lord shows the way to follow in preference to any of these other ways.*

When Philip discovered that the Messianic prophecies of the Old Testament converged on Jesus of Nazareth, he told Nathanael, "We have found him, of whom Moses in the law, and the prophets, did write, Jesus of Nazareth." John 1:45.

Even so, as we see how these six concurrent prophecies converge on the Sabbath reform movement of Seventh-day Adventism, we can with Biblical certainty say, We have found the repairers of the breach of whom Isaiah prophesied. We have found those who, at the end of the 2300 days of Daniel 8:12-14, are restoring the truth that was cast to the ground. We have found those who will receive the seal of God as they keep the seventh day as the sign of God, their Creator and Redeemer. (Revelation 7:1-3.) We have found the "remnant" who keep the commandments of God and have the testimony of Jesus. (Revelation 12:17.) We have found the people of God's threefold message of Revelation 14:6-12.

"This is the Lord's doing; it is marvellous in our eyes. This is the day which the Lord hath made; we will rejoice and be glad in it." Psalm 118:23, 24.

Yet the sure word of prophecy not only forecasts how this final gospel and Sabbath reform movement would be inaugurated in 1844; it also describes how it would develop into a world movement that would march on into eternal triumph on the sea of glass before God's throne.

"And I saw as it were a sea of glass mingled with fire:

and them that had gotten the victory over the beast, and over his image, and over his mark, and over the number of his name, stand on the sea of glass, having the harps of God.

"And they sing the song of Moses the servant of God, and the song of the Lamb, saying, Great and marvellous are thy works, Lord God Almighty; just and true are thy ways, thou King of saints." Revelation 15:2, 3.

In vision John saw the second coming of Christ after the threefold message had been proclaimed in all the world. (Revelation 14:14-20.) And God will gather to heaven all the righteous from all lands and from all the generations of mankind at the second advent of Christ. (Matthew 24:30, 31; 1 Thessalonians 4:16, 17.) Then after Christ's return, John saw a special company who "had gotten the victory over the beast, and over his image, and over his mark," standing before God's throne.

Who are they? Where did they come from? Revelation 14:6-20 and 15:2, 3 show that they are the people belonging to God's threefold-message movement who have kept the commandments of God and the faith of Jesus. They have gotten the victory over the beast, his image, and his mark as mentioned in this threefold message and will go through to eternal victory in heaven.

Scripture shows that the same movement which proclaims the threefold message to every nation will sweep forward without a break to eternal victory in heaven at the coming of the Lord. *This is the divinely appointed destiny of the Advent Movement—a most impelling and decisive reason to accept the threefold message and stay by it to the end.*

God's last message to all men is being preached around the world in eight hundred languages and dialects. Honest men and women who desire above everything else to obey the Lord Jesus Christ and to follow Him all the way are becoming convinced of Bible truth and are taking their stand for keeping the commandments of God and the faith of Jesus. Several hundred thousand each year unite with this threefold-message movement—the wisest and best decision any soul can make.

A signboard on the road to the left says, "The first day of the week is the Sabbath or Lord's day by the agreement of men." We look down that road and see millions of people going that way. A signboard on the road to the right says, "The seventh day is the Sabbath or Lord's day by the sanctification and commandment of the Lord Jesus Christ." When we look down that road, we see only a few people traveling on it.

On the side of Sunday we see the bishops, priests, and popes of Rome as well as thousands of Protestant ministers, many of whom have never searched the Bible regarding the Sabbath question. We see millions of good church members who take it for granted that Sunday-keeping is Biblical.

On the side of the seventh day we see Abraham, Moses, Elijah, Daniel, David, Isaiah, Jeremiah, Ezekiel, all the prophets, John the Baptist, Peter, James, John, Paul, all the apostles, and the Apostolic Church.

We see the concurrent testimony of six prophecies of a Sabbath reform movement in this time-of-the-end period. We hear God calling for repairers of the breach. We hear Him ask, "Who is on the Lord's side for keeping the commandments of God and the faith of Jesus?"

We look down to the end of the road for those who keep this seventh day and see them standing on the sea of glass. A figure towers above them all, Jesus of Nazareth. He raises His nail-pierced hands and beckons us to come, and we cry out, "Jesus, we take our stand with You in truly observing the seventh day."

THE FINAL TEST

When we consider the trend of events, with the prophecies of Revelation 13 and 14 as the background, we see that the affairs of men are shaping up for the final crisis, which will usher in the close of human probation. It is of the utmost importance that everyone thoroughly understand this final test.

According to Revelation 7:1-3, God invites everybody to receive His seal, or sign, in his forehead. On the other hand, the beast power will attempt to impose its mark, or sign, upon everyone. Thus the final test involves the reception of the seal of God versus the reception of the mark of the beast. And it is self-evident that the seal of God represents the side of truth and obedience while the mark of the beast stands for the opposite—disobedience and error.

We cannot mistake the seal of God. Four times in the

Word Christ declares that the seventh-day Sabbath is a sign or seal. (Exodus 31:13, 16, 17; Ezekiel 20:12, 20.) So the conclusion is clear. Since the mark of the beast is the opposite of the seal of God, it involves keeping the man-made sabbath which apostate Christendom has established in the place of Christ's true Sabbath.

Many seals contain three points of information: the name of the one using the seal, his title, and his territory. Check over the Ten Commandments one by one. Where alone do we find the constituents of a seal? The second, third, and fifth contain the name "Lord thy God," but only the Sabbath commandment forever distinguishes the true God from all false gods. This commandment bears the vital constituents of a seal: (1) the name, "Lord thy God"; (2) the distinguishing title, "The Lord made heaven and earth" —the Creator; the territory, "heaven and earth." Thus the Sabbath commandment imparts validity to the other nine precepts. It is the seal of God's law and the sign of Christ's total supremacy. Hence, receiving the seal of God must involve keeping His Sabbath.

Will all who keep the seventh day receive this seal of God for heaven? No, because there is a right way and a wrong way to keep the Sabbath. Receiving God's seal involves proper Sabbathkeeping as a sign of continuing personal sanctification. Revelation 7:2-4 and 14:1 confirm this. Being sealed with God's seal is identical with having the Father's name written upon the forehead. The forehead represents the mind. The Father's name signifies His character. Thus, when the seal of God is placed upon a person, it signifies that the character of Christ has been reproduced in him, that the person has fully surrendered to God's will in every area of his life.

The seal of any government incorporates some distinctive design that has been chosen as a sign of its authority.

Christ has chosen the seventh-day Sabbath as the sign of His authority. It represents the seal of the living God.

The mark of the beast, on the other hand, pertains to the Sunday institution of the papal power as the sign of its alleged authority to rule Christians in religious matters. The Roman Catholic Church declares that changing the day of rest from Saturday to Sunday marks its power to rule in religious matters.

An official catechism known as *An Abridgment of the Christian Doctrine,* by the Rev. Henry Tuberville, page 58, poses this question and answer:

"Ques.—How prove you that the church hath power to command feasts and holy days?"

"Ans.—By the very act of changing the Sabbath into Sunday." (Emphasis supplied.)

The Bible reveals only one way to escape receiving the mark of the beast—to keep the commandments of God and the faith of Jesus as pointed out in the very next verse after the warning against the mark of the beast.

Everyone needs to ask himself, "Will I, by God's grace, so keep the true Sabbath that I will stand among those John saw on the sea of glass in heaven with victory over the mark of the beast?"

The issue of the seal of God versus the mark of the beast reduces itself to this: Those who keep the seventh-day Sabbath as Christ commands are distinguished as His followers; those who keep the first-day sabbath of the Papacy are distinguished as its followers.

The New Testament emphasizes that by obedience or disobedience to the commandments each believer shows whether or not he is a real Christian. "And hereby we do know that we know him, if we keep his commandments. He that saith, I know him, and keepeth not his commandments, is a liar, and the truth is not in him." 1 John 2:3, 4.

The issue of obedience determines on which side you and I stand in the conflict of the ages between Christ and Satan. Thus the Word of God lays down this decisive principle: "Whom ye . . . obey, his servants ye are." Romans 6:16.

When a Christian keeps the seventh day as the divinely appointed sign that Christ is the Lord and Creator-Redeemer, whom does he obey in this? The Bible answers, The Lord Jesus Christ. Hence, he is Christ's servant.

When a Christian keeps Sunday, whom is he obeying? Many honestly think they are obeying Christ because He arose from the dead on this day, but according to the Bible, Jesus never asked anyone to keep the first day of the week for any reason. When a Christian keeps Sunday, he obeys the Catholic power, which attempted to change the Sabbath from Saturday to Sunday. He is its servant, and Sunday-keeping stands as a mark of his obedience to it above Christ in this matter of the Sabbath. He has honored the Papacy as another god above the Lord.

In the final test every soul will have to make his choice between Christ's true Sabbath and the spurious sabbath of the antichrist. Satan will work through a world church-state union to impose the false sabbath upon all. Thus we read, "And he causeth all, both small and great, rich and poor, free and bond, to receive a mark in their right hand, or in their foreheads: and that no man might buy or sell, save he that had the mark, or the name of the beast, or the number of his name." Revelation 13:16, 17.

All will obey this apostate power and receive the mark of the beast except Christ's "remnant," who keep the commandments of God and the faith of Jesus. (Revelation 13:8.) Christ's "remnant" will be all that prevents Satan from imposing his false system upon the entire world. If he could wipe them out, his triumph would be complete. So a decree will go forth that all who refuse to keep the false sabbath should be killed. (Revelation 13:15.)

So here is the final test. The world powers will decree that no one can buy or sell unless he has the mark of the beast, and finally that all who will not worship the beast and his image and receive his mark should be killed. On the other hand, God, to whom every soul will give account, declares, "If any man worship the beast and his image, and receive his mark, . . . the same shall drink of the wine of the wrath of God; . . . and he shall be tormented with fire and brimstone." Revelation 14:9, 10.

What a test! It resembles the test which came to the three Hebrew young men in Babylon. (See Daniel 3.) God wonderfully delivered them. Even so He will deliver His remnant from the death decree of Satan. (Daniel 12:1; Joel 2:32; Revelation 3:10.)

If a person does not voluntarily surrender all to Christ to keep His true Sabbath and receive His seal, he will be compelled by civil law to honor the false sabbath and receive the mark of the beast.

Many dismiss this Sabbath-versus-Sunday issue as being of no consequence. They think it is only a matter of argumentation, but God's warning message in Revelation 14:9-12 identifies the real issue. Shall we show our acceptance of Christ's total supremacy by keeping His true Sabbath? Or shall we keep Sunday and thereby accept the alleged supremacy of the Catholic power? Whom shall we obey as supreme—God or man?

14

DIVINE WONDER-WORKING

"The eyes of the Lord run to and fro throughout the whole earth, to shew himself strong in the behalf of them whose heart is perfect toward him." 2 Chronicles 16:9. God is searching through all the billions of people on earth for those who really desire to know the truth so that they may obey it. He works to bring the person who wants the truth in contact with His message so that he can know, believe, and obey.

The treasurer of Ethiopia, while riding in his chariot on the Gaza road south of Jerusalem, was reading from what is now known as the fifty-third chapter of Isaiah. He was deeply stirred to know the meaning of this prophecy when a man appeared beside the chariot who knew its meaning. The treasurer asked him to share this knowledge with him.

It was no mere coincidence that this treasurer was reading from Isaiah 53. No other place in all the Old Testament could so effectively and quickly bring him into a living union with the crucified Christ as his personal Saviour.

Then there was the precise timing of the Holy Spirit's alerting of Philip to take the right direction on this road to contact a searcher for truth. The Lord guided Philip to make the right approach for securing an opening to unfold the truth, and the right results followed.

A newborn son of God sealed his acceptance of the Lamb of God by baptism and went on his way rejoicing in the truth, ready to tell others what a Friend he had found in Jesus. We see a divine wonder-working through it all. A sincere man seeking truth comes into contact with one of God's people who has the truth to pass on to him. The eyes of the Lord do run to and fro in all the earth to show Himself strong in behalf of those whose hearts are sincere before Him.

It is truly marvelous how God works at both ends of the line to bring sincere souls into His truth. Acts 10 reveals how God worked at both ends of a thirty-mile stretch of road from Caesarea to Joppa. The divine hand precisely timed and simultaneously prepared Cornelius and Peter for the needed contact. God guided him who had the truth to the centurion who sought more truth.

Peter's vision came exactly at the right moment to prepare him to receive the messengers from Cornelius. In fact, the climax of the vision came just when the messengers arrived. The timing of the vision of Cornelius with that of Peter was so ordered of God as to permit the arrival of the messengers at Peter's lodging at exactly the right moment—not too early, not too late. God ordered everything so that a sincere soul seeking for more truth could receive it from one of His people who knew that truth.

The question arises, Why didn't the Lord have the angel

who appeared to Cornelius unfold the truth that he needed above all else? God honors the ministry He has established and works through those who compose His church. He plans that those who accept His truth shall come in contact with His church and connect with it.

The Book of Acts makes it very clear that God does guide those who determine to do His will, but it also shows that God guides the organized body of His followers who make up His church.

Since God directs both parties, neither one will be arrayed against the other. God will not guide an individual contrary to the way in which He is leading His church.

A young man was sitting in his Sunday School class at the Methodist church. The lesson for that morning was based on Exodus 20:3-17—the record of the Ten Commandments which the Lord spoke from heaven at Sinai.

Two days before that Sunday, a Sabbathkeeping book salesman had stopped at the home of a certain steward of that church. They studied the Bible for several hours regarding the Sabbath. At midnight the Methodist deacon arose from his chair and with intense earnestness resolved, "God helping me, I will never work on another Saturday. I am determined to keep Christ's true Sabbath."

So he kept his first Sabbath. The next day he went to the Methodist church on the Sunday just mentioned. In the absence of the regular teacher of the young men's class, he taught the lesson dealing with the Ten Commandments. Naturally, having just kept his first Sabbath, he shared his new belief when these young Methodists came to the statement—"The seventh day is the sabbath of the Lord."

As a result, the young man in the class also began to keep the seventh day as the Lord Jesus directs in His commandment. He, in turn, has heralded the Sabbath message from coast to coast, and thousands have accepted it.

Certain questions come to the forefront here: How did it happen that on that particular Sunday the lesson dealt with the Ten Commandments? How did it happen that the regular teacher of the young men's class was absent? How did it happen that in her absence the superintendent asked this particular deacon to teach the class? How did it happen that he had just kept his first Sabbath? How did it happen that the Christian door-to-door salesman came to his house on the Friday prior to this Sunday and had led him by a Bible study to keep his first Sabbath? God was at work to prepare one of the many heralds of His last-day Sabbath-reform message.

The great Father, who loves all mankind, is searching among earth's millions to reveal Himself to every man, woman, boy, and girl who is willing and determined to do His will. Thus Jesus said, "If any man will do his will, he shall know of the doctrine." John 7:17. God will bring such people into a blessed fellowship with Himself, His Son, and the Holy Spirit. This in turn will transform and perfect their characters to live forever in His coming kingdom of glory. Amazing transformations that are almost incredible are being effected in the hearts and lives of those who respond to the call of the Lord and obey Him.

God is searching for every person who will follow His truth above every other consideration. Will God find the object of His quest in you and in me? Everything else in the world sinks into insignificance in contrast to the blessed and eternal results that come from following His truth.

We could compile a book of the marvelous workings of God as He seeks people in every land to lead them into His truth. There is, today, story after story akin to these we have considered from the Acts of the Apostles and the story of the young Sunday School scholar. Truly "God moves in a mysterious way His wonders to perform."

God's eye watches every sincere person to show Himself strong in the Christian's behalf.

"Every one that is of the truth heareth [or heedeth] my voice." "My sheep hear my voice, . . . and they follow me." "He that is of God heareth God's words: ye therefore hear them not, because ye are not of God." (John 18:37; 10:27; 8:47.)

Regardless of how far apart two lines may be at their beginning, if each has a continuous slight slant toward the other, they will finally merge. So it is with the sincere heart and God's truth. The sincere heart is looking for the truth. The truth is looking for the truly sincere. The truth and the sincere heart will come together in blessed union.

Keeping the Sabbath often presents a real test of one's faith. A man sees that it is right and knows he ought to keep it, but he says, "If I don't report on Saturday, I will lose my job." Or, "If I close my business on Saturday, I will lose out." It is a real test of faith.

But faith can and does make a way where there seems to be no way. Jesus said, "According to your faith be it unto you." "As thou hast believed, so be it done unto thee." "If thou canst believe, all things are possible to him that believeth." Matthew 9:29; 8:13; Mark 9:23.

"If ye have faith as a grain of mustard seed, ye shall say unto this mountain, Remove hence to yonder place; and it shall remove; and nothing shall be impossible unto you." Matthew 17:20.

"If ye have faith as a grain of mustard seed." The Bible declares that it is one of the smallest of seeds. So the smallest faith can remove mountains—not literal mountains of dirt or stone but mountains of difficulty. (Compare Zechariah 4:7.) Faith can remove those obstacles which seem to prevent a person from moving forward to keep the Sabbath.

In a certain city a railroad dispatcher heard the message

about the true Sabbath and was fully persuaded that he
ought to begin keeping it. When he asked for Saturdays off,
the superintendent of the division replied, "The railroad
knows no Sabbath. Unless you report on Saturdays, you have
no job here." His faith stood the test, however, and he began
to keep the Sabbath in the face of losing his job.

Here was a mountain in his path for making a living and
obeying the Sabbath commandment, but he had faith as a
grain of mustard seed. He made a trip to a distant city to
talk to the president of this great rail system and presented
his case.

Impressed, the president called the division superintendent and directed him to reinstate this man to his former
job and to give him Saturdays off. The Sabbathkeeper's faith
had removed the mountain.

When the ten lepers moved forward by faith to be
checked by the priest, what happened? "As they went, they
were cleansed." (Luke 17:11-14.)

When the man who had been paralyzed for thirty-eight
years asserted his faith by attempting to rise and walk, he
was made whole. (John 5:1-9.)

When the Israelites moved forward by faith to cross the
Jordan, God parted the waters, and they walked across on a
dry riverbed. (Joshua 3.)

So we must have faith in God; and if we move forward
in faith to keep Christ's Sabbath, He will make a way for us.
Faith in action releases God's power for victory.